Building
a Team

Building a Team

the practical guide to mastering management

DeeDee Doke, Mike Bourne, Pippa Bourne, Phillip L. Hunsaker,
Johanna S. Hunsaker

Material previously published in
Interviewing People, Motivating People, Managing People

London, New York,
Munich, Melbourne, Delhi

Project Editor: Daniel Mills
Project Designer: Isabel de Cordova
Managing Editor: Penny Warren
Managing Art Editor: Glenda Fisher
Production Editor: Ben Marcus
Senior Production Controller: Man Fai Lau
Creative Technical Support: Sonia Charbonnier
Publisher: Peggy Vance
US Editor: Liza Kaplan

First American Edition, 2011
Published in the United States by
DK Publishing, 375 Hudson Street
New York, New York 10014

11 12 13 14 15   10 9 8 7 6 5 4 3 2 1
178910—January 2011

Material previously published in: *Interviewing
People, Motivating People, Managing People.*

Published in Great Britain by Dorling Kindersley
Limited. A catalogue record for this book is
available from the Library of Congress.
ISBN: 978-0-7566-6859-4

DK books are available at special discounts
when purchased in bulk for sales promotions,
premiums, fund-raising, or educational use.
For details, contact: DK Publishing Special
Markets, 375 Hudson Street, New York,
New York 10014 or SpecialSales@dk.com.

Color reproduction by Alta Images, London
Printed and bound in China by Starlite

Discover more at
www.dk.com

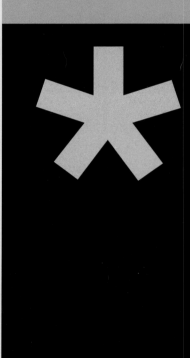

Contents

8   INTERVIEWING PEOPLE

Chapter 1
Planning the interview

12   Developing a checklist
14   Creating the job description
18   Using digital aids
20   Creating a matrix
22   Deciding on the agenda
24   Building the shortlist
26   Inviting the candidates

Chapter 2
Conducting the interview

28   Setting the tone
30   Choosing the format
32   Competency-based questions
34   Asking further questions
36   Respecting diversity
38   Avoiding illegal questions
40   Effective observation
42   Concluding the interview

Chapter 3
Supplementing the interview

44   Gathering further information
46   Holding an assessment center
48   Using psychometric tests
50   Testing skills and ability
52   Conducting group activities
56   Background screening
58   Using social networking sites

Chapter 4
Making the final decision

60   Aligning goals
62   Assessing strengths
66   Making the offer
68   Obtaining references
70   Sending rejection letters
72   Reviewing your process
74   Onboarding new employees

Chapter 1
Creating a motivating environment

80   Supporting performance
82   Principles of motivation
86   Creating the right conditions
88   Creating a high-performance culture
90   Recruiting the right people
92   Measuring motivation

Chapter 2
Building processes for motivation

94   Designing a job role
96   Creating a balance
98   Conducting appraisals
100   Setting objectives
104   Measuring progress
106   Training and development
108   Recognizing performance
110   Paying for performance

Chapter 3
Developing the skills of motivation

112   Motivating yourself
116   Being a good motivator
118   Making people feel valued
120   Developing communication
122   Identifying demotivation
124   Consulting others
126   Delegating effectively
128   Coaching successfully

Chapter 4
Motivating in difficult situations

130   Motivating during change
134   Motivating dispersed workers
136   Motivating underperformers
138   Motivating a project team
140   Motivating teams
142   Bringing it all together

144 MANAGING PEOPLE

Chapter 1
Understanding yourself

148 Developing self-awareness
150 Using emotional intelligence
152 Applying assertiveness
154 Examining your assumptions
156 Clarifying your values
158 Developing your personal
mission statement

Chapter 2
Interacting with others

160 Communicating effectively
162 Sending messages
164 Listening actively
166 Reading nonverbal cues
168 Teaching skills
170 Giving feedback
172 Negotiating
174 Managing conflict
176 Valuing diversity

Chapter 3
Managing a team

178 Setting goals and planning
180 Designing work
182 High-performing teams
186 Delegating effectively
188 Motivating others
192 Appraising performance

Chapter 4
Leading others

194 Setting ethical boundaries
196 Ensuring cultural fit
198 Solving problems
200 Building power
202 Managing change
204 Helping others improve
208 Coaching and mentoring
210 Managing careers

212 Index
222 Author Biographies
224 Acknowledgments

INTERVIEWING
PEOPLE

Contents

10 Introduction

CHAPTER 1
Planning the interview

12 Developing a checklist
14 Creating the job description
18 Using digital aids
20 Creating a matrix
22 Deciding on the agenda
24 Building the shortlist
26 Inviting the candidates

CHAPTER 2
Conducting the interview

28 Setting the tone
30 Choosing the format
32 Competency-based questions
34 Asking further questions
36 Respecting diversity
38 Avoiding illegal questions
40 Effective observation
42 Concluding the interview

CHAPTER 3
Supplementing the interview

44 Gathering further information
46 Holding an assessment center
48 Using psychometric tests
50 Testing skills and ability
52 Conducting group activities
56 Background screening
58 Using social networking sites

CHAPTER 4
Making the final decision

60 Aligning goals
62 Assessing strengths
66 Making the offer
68 Obtaining references
70 Sending rejection letters
72 Reviewing your process
74 Onboarding new employees

Introduction

The key to success for any organization is its people. Getting the right people depends on how an organization recruits, and a fundamental element of the recruitment process is interviewing.

As the business environment becomes more dynamic, organizations' needs change, and so do the skills they require of their employees. Moreover, simply having the right skills does not guarantee a candidate will benefit your organization. Today's most creative and progressive recruiters recognize that understanding the aptitudes, attitudes, and motivations of their employees is essential in making sure that the people they hire represent the best possible fit for current vacancies. As a result, those who conduct job interviews on behalf of their organizations not only hold the present, but also the future of their employer squarely in their hands. That is a lot of responsibility.

The goal of *Interviewing People* is to guide you through the minefield of interviewing candidates: organizing the interviews and other supplementary activities; helping you ask the right questions; deciding which information sources you should consider in finding out who the person really is; and preparing the groundwork for successful partnerships between the new employees and your organization. The end result should be to make interviews rewarding for candidates and recruiters.

Chapter 1
Planning the interview

Interviewing a potential recruit is a long and complex process, but the reward is seeing the person you interviewed contributing to your organization's success and happy in their job. Achieving that success takes careful planning.

Developing a checklist

Your checklist is your step-by-step guide to making sure that you and your organization make the most of the candidate interviews. Create it at the very beginning of your recruitment process so you can always visualize where you are at a given moment and what you need to do next.

TIP

PLAN UNTIL THE END

Include time in your plan to check references and make an offer once you have chosen a candidate.

Planning to plan

Preparing for and conducting an interview involves a number of steps. However, the actual interview is only one part of the process. Your checklist should cover the steps required before the interview, during the interview, and afterward. Your plan should also incorporate points along the way at which you assess progress to date and make any necessary amendments. Leave room to add extra stages if necessary. Remember, it won't always be possible to execute each step perfectly. Concentrate on fulfilling each point and keep a record of what you do and the results.

Breaking it down into steps

First, analyze and understand the job itself and its significance in your organization. Next, map out the steps of your strategy for filling it: where you will publicize the vacancy; what support you will need to screen and rank incoming résumés; how to define your short list; the kinds of questions to be asked of candidates at interview; and selecting any other measures that would be required to supplement the interviews. Then there will be logistics issues to be worked out, such as where the interviews will be held.

TIP

SOLICIT EMPLOYEE REFERRALS
Reward employees for recommending friends and relatives for jobs in your organization. The new employee gets recognition, and the organization gets a well recommended new employee.

Budgeting for your strategy

Know what your budget is from the start; finances play a role in identifying top, secondary, and optional priorities on your checklist. One key spend is likely to be on recruitment advertising. Renting a venue for interviews and getting expert help to assess candidates' skills may also mean spending some money. Get estimates on every expenditure before you spend anything.

✔ CHECKLIST **PRE-INTERVIEW PLANNING**

	YES	NO
• Do I understand the job and where it fits in my organization?	☐	☐
• Have I planned a recruitment/interview/assessment budget?	☐	☐
• Have I decided whether supplementary meetings, such as assessment centers, are necessary?	☐	☐
• Have I placed the recruitment advertisements in appropriate media?	☐	☐
• Have I considered meeting places and venues for interviews?	☐	☐
• Have I designed the questions?	☐	☐
• Have I decided on the interview format (panel or pair, for example)?	☐	☐
• Have I fit in reassessment times to look back at what I have accomplished to date and consider what needs to be done next?	☐	☐

Creating the job description

The job profile starts by acting as a sort of recipe for the person you are looking for, but comes to define expectations of the job holder as well as aspects of your organization's purpose. The profile reveals one individual piece of how your organization sees its future.

TIP

LOOK AHEAD
Make sure the job description gives the role context in terms of the organization and the types of challenges and growth opportunities provided.

Setting the "rules of the game"

A well thought out job description can help attract candidates who are right for the job. It also serves as a foundation for appraisals and employee development plans, and it outlines for both job holder and manager the "rules of the game" in day-to-day activities and over the long term. The person specification, which is often part of the job description, defines the kinds of education, experience, skills, and personal characteristics that are likely to be necessary to succeed in the job.

ASK YOURSELF...
WHAT ARE THE JOB REQUIREMENTS

- Why does this job exist?
- What must this job holder achieve for the organization?
- Which responsibilities could be reallocated to allow the addition of new ones?
- What changes are planned for the organization that could affect this job?
- What skills should the job holder have to make the organizational transition easier?

Analyzing your needs

You may be filling an existing job that has just been vacated. A vacancy provides an opportunity to consider the continuing need for the job. If a need remains, then examine whether the role demands the inclusion of new responsibilities, competencies, and knowledge. Keep in mind that as organizations evolve, their needs and strategy change, and so must the dimensions of the work and the jobs created to carry out that work. Think about how your organization is changing and its impact on the role.

Defining the job's purpose

The starting point for both creating and refreshing a job description or profile is defining the job's purpose. What is the main reason for the job's existence and what is the job holder expected to achieve? From there, go on to construct the description's skeleton, which must include the following: job title, main duties and responsibilities, who the job holder reports to, who reports to the job holder, where the job is based, and whether it is full-time, part-time, or flexi-time. Use the profile to build a compelling case for the job's desirability, such as responsibility for certain projects.

Sharing the full picture

One of the job description's purposes is to attract applicants. It can be tempting to exaggerate the most interesting aspects of the role and downplay the least interesting. Misrepresenting the job role does no one any favors. Highlight the job's best points, but balance the description so applicants understand the full picture of what the role entails. Be truthful, skip the jargon, and write as clear and concise a description as possible.

Creating the person specification

Developing a precise person specification requires an in-depth understanding of the competencies, knowledge, skills, experience, education, aptitudes, and attitudes the best possible selected hire for this role could have. Break requirements down into "essential" and "desirable" categories, which can help differentiate between candidates when the time comes to build your short list. Focus on qualitative aspects of experience instead of an arbitrary number of years or qualifications. Perhaps the most challenging part of creating the person specification is effectively building in personal characteristics that are desirable or necessary in the job holder. Recognize that you will need to link interview questions to the person specification, as well as the job description, so consider also how a candidate can best demonstrate to you that they have, for instance, "integrity" or "initiative." Never use terms that are discriminatory, such as "mature," "bright, young college graduate," "Christian values," and so on.

7 EXPLAIN SPECIAL CONDITIONS
Detail conditions, such as working unusual shifts or on public holidays, regular travel, or wearing a particular uniform.

6 DESCRIBE THE SCOPE OF THE JOB
Explain the boundaries of the job holder's responsibilities and the potential for developing them further.

1 DEFINE THE JOB PURPOSE
Ask yourself what the person filling this role is supposed to accomplish. This step influences the rest of the process.

2 IDENTIFY THE JOB TITLE
The job's purpose sets out what the role should be called. Keep the job title free of jargon, brief, and as clear as possible.

Developing a job profile to fit your requirements

3 DESCRIBE THE CONTEXT
Refer to the work conditions and nature of the business in which the job duties will be performed.

4 OUTLINE THE JOB'S OBJECTIVES
Specify the key goals, for example, provide efficient customer service that ensures problems are dealt with effectively.

5 SET OUT THE BASICS OF THE JOB
Outline the day-to-day responsibilities and tasks, the skills needed to fulfill the job duties, and hours required weekly.

Using digital aids

Interviewing is a person-to-person interaction. However, technology can be a valuable ally in today's recruitment process. You can put technology to work for you early on to advertise your job via your corporate website or on job boards. Then well-chosen recruitment software can be used to screen and organize the field of candidates who apply.

Maximizing your brand

Your organization's website is often the first port of call for two sets of job seekers. The first group knows of your organization and is interested in finding out what it would be like to work there and if there are currently any vacancies. The second is taking a look after seeing an advertisement for the job on offer. If your organization has the resources, its site should offer a careers section that features full job/person descriptions and online tools that allow candidates to upload résumés. Some organizations upload videos of current employees explaining what it is like to work there on their site. Other organizations showcase written testimonials and photographs. If you can't afford "bells and whistles," make sure at a minimum that it is easy to find up-to-date job listings on the site.

TAP INTO SOCIAL MEDIA
Build your own profile on a professional social media networking site to help attract potential candidates.

Using social media

Going online takes your recruitment effort into a whole new cyber realm. Savvy managers and recruiters turn to professional social networking sites like LinkedIn, Naymz, and Plaxo to reach "passive" job seekers (those who are not looking for jobs at the moment) and to spread the word that a job is available. To get the most out of such sites, join subgroups that can broaden your outreach—by location, industry, or profession.

Using job boards

The use of online job boards* as a recruitment tool for all kinds of jobs is increasing rapidly. The generalist job board may be the right vehicle to get the word out about entry-level and less specialized types of roles, but career professionals tend to seek out the niche job boards. Although job boards specializing in vacancies for senior executives are growing in popularity, they do not attract as much interest from qualified applicants as online services aimed at more junior professionals. You may want to post your vacancy on more than one job board to increase its visibility.

*Job board—an online service on which employers can post details of vacancies for a fee.

Tracking candidates

Depending on your organization's size and the number of people hired each year, software that helps manage the recruitment process from beginning to end may be a worthwhile investment. Widely known as applicant tracking systems (ATS), recruitment software can deliver services from posting job notices and importing candidates' online job applications to screening résumés, scheduling interviews, managing your communications with candidates, and more.

TIP

KNOW YOUR OPTIONS
Investigate a variety of recruitment software. Systems have been created specifically for large or small organizations.

CASE STUDY

Streamlining applications
British airline bmi increased the number of job applications it handled over a six-month period by 25 percent by putting into place recruitment and talent-management software. The airline often received hundreds of applications a week, but had only a few employees working in its recruitment department.

Paperwork constituted a major part of the team's workload because applicants would first send in a résumé and would then be sent an application form. The company saved thousands of dollars in printing and postage costs by taking its application process online. The online system also allowed more efficient screening of candidates.

Creating a matrix

Interviewing can become a very subjective process because it involves people, and their impressions and interpretations of information and how it is delivered. You can remove some of the subjectivity by building a framework that gives context to the relative importance of candidates' education, experience, skills, and key personal qualities.

Constructing a filtering matrix

Devising a matrix to filter the flow of candidates in the early stage of selection will save processing time. It consists of a list of candidates running down one side, and a list of minimum and preferred education, professional experience, and skills requirements running along the top. The requirements listed on the matrix should match those in the job posting. A simple "yes/no" or check-box system is best for indicating whether or not the requirements have been met. Ultimately, the filtering matrix is the document supporting the decision to interview, or not interview, a particular candidate.

Charting a qualitative matrix

DEVELOP A POINTS SYSTEM

Decide before the actual interviews what different scores will mean in your interviewing matrix. For instance, if the top score for a given area is five, what must a candidate demonstrate to be scored at five?

An interview will require you to score candidates on information that is less factual and more qualitative in nature, so a matrix for this stage will reflect the quality of a response rather than a simple yes or no. The areas you measure will be personal qualities, such as communication skills, business awareness, and knowledge. Each will receive points with, say, a top score of five. You may want to "weight" particular areas, by either raising the top score or by multiplying the given score by a number to reflect that area's importance to the hiring decision. You can use the same basic visual framework design as the filtering matrix.

Adding it all up

Organize your matrices so that information is readily accessible and your scoring system for each is easily understandable. Then create a single score sheet that outlines the accumulated score from each activity of the interviewing process for each candidate. Once you have completed interviewing and assessing your candidates, add up the scores to see which candidate has come out on top. If a question arises over selection later on, a transparent system will support and clarify your decision and the process used to make your choice.

TIP

EXAMINE ALL AREAS
Keep in mind that if you incorporate complex activities in your interview process, an additional matrix will be necessary to reflect candidates' performance there as well.

Sample of a qualitative matrix

SCORING SYSTEM:
1—No evidence of competency
2—Limited competency (one example)
3—Acceptable (meets the minimum standard for the job)
4—Significant (examples demonstrate confidence)
5—Extensive (many excellent examples that reflect well-rounded professional knowledge and expertise)

CANDIDATES	COMMUNICATION SKILLS	INDUSTRY KNOWLEDGE	TECHNICAL KNOWLEDGE	REGIONAL KNOWLEDGE	TOTAL SCORE
Candidate 1	3	3	3	3	12
Candidate 2	5	4	4	5	18
Candidate 3	2	3	3	4	12
Candidate 4	4	5	5	3	17

Deciding on the agenda

To make the most of your interview, you need a plan that sets out not only the informational ground you want to cover, but also outlines the time you want to devote to each segment of the interview. Your agenda should also include any "extras" that the interview process must incorporate.

Bringing the elements together

The question-and-answer segment of getting to know your candidates is referred to as "the interview," but to get the most out of your exposure to them, think instead of the interview as a multipart event that may require several different settings and techniques. The core points to decide are whether you will have a single interview or first and second interviews, and if supplementary activities should be included. For example, when candidates come in for interviews, a tour of your facility may be appropriate to give them an idea of what the work environment is like and to show them employee facilities. It will also give you a chance to see their spontaneous reactions to the environment.

Organizing your time

TIP

BUILD IN IN-BETWEEN TIME

Pleasantries take time, so be sure to plan in enough time to welcome each candidate as they arrive, and to say goodbye—and when they might expect to hear from you— as they depart.

How long each interview should last will depend on the amount of information you must obtain from each candidate. This will be based on the complexity of the role or the seniority of the position. However, you should allow at least 45–60 minutes for the question-and-answer portion of an in-person interview. Reviewing the job description and person specifications is a good starting point for developing the questions. Use it also to plan the pace of your interview by deciding how much time should be devoted to each segment, based on its importance to your selection criteria.

Planning for contingencies

The best-laid plans can go awry when the unexpected occurs. Your interviews could be thrown off kilter by late arrivals, office emergencies, or any number of everyday events. Work out a "Plan B" to help you and your candidates navigate smoothly through any problems that could occur on the day of the interview. One common contingency is running behind schedule, which can threaten the goodwill of your remaining candidates throughout the day as well as raise the possibility you won't get all the information you want during the interview. Perhaps the room you've arranged as the interview location has been double booked. A candidate, or you, could be faced with a personal emergency. Develop a list of "what ifs" in order to plan effective solutions for a range of contingencies.

Building the short list

The list of candidates who will be invited to the interview will form your short list. Following the interview, you may trim this list even more to choose some to participate in further selection activities in your search for the best possible candidate.

Selecting the best

Build your interview short list with the help of the filtering matrix, which will make it clear which applicants met most of your requirements and which did not. Your next steps depend on two factors: how many applicants met most or all of the minimum and preferred requirements, and how many people you want to interview for the job. If your list does not include the desired number of candidates to interview, look at the applicants who met the highest percentage of the minimum requirements. Examine their résumés for individual differentiators, such as evidence of promotions, recent training, or unpaid work experience.

Achieving a manageable short list

Work with at least one other person to develop your short list to eliminate the possibility of bias. For a manageable list, keep in mind how much time you will have to devote to interviews. A short list for a senior or complex role should be small because there will be few people with the right blend of skills, experience, and personal qualities who meet highly specific requirements. Too many applicants for a high-level role indicates that the job advertisement may have been written too broadly.

If you are hiring in volume, consider initial telephone screening to help you narrow your short list to interview. Telephone screening can also be useful for confirming the candidates' credentials, probing gaps in employment history, exploring their willingness to relocate, or determining whether their salary expectations are in line with what your organization is prepared to offer. Telephone screening can save money and time by eliminating unqualified or inappropriate applicants from the short list to interview.

TIP

USE MULTIPLE SHORT LISTS
Consider ranking the candidates in separate categories, based on key priorities for the job, for example, professional skill, management experience, and education. Then invite the top two in each list for the interview.

Considering the overqualified

As a recruiting manager you may face the difficult task of deciding whether a job will sufficiently challenge and stimulate a potential employee. Some organizations disfavor overqualified candidates because of concerns they might get bored or will cost too much. Other employers look at hiring such candidates as an opportunity to develop a role and, possibly, a team or the entire organization in new ways. If you have seemingly overqualified applicants on your short list, ask yourself what their impact would be in a particular job role.

Inviting the candidates

Extend the invitation to a job interview with the same enthusiasm with which you hope your candidates receive it. Be clear in the information you provide, and prepare to adapt your plans if some candidates require special assistance.

TIP

ADDRESS WITH CARE

Address candidates by first names instead of Mr. or Ms. initially, to avoid embarrassment over gender-neutral names.

Personalizing the invitation

An invitation to attend an interview is the first personalized communication you will send a candidate, and it must accomplish several things. It should provide information, get across a sense of your organization's style and culture, and communicate pleasure that the candidate has chosen to apply for this role. Using phrases like "I am pleased to invite you," "We look forward to meeting you," or "Your experience interested us greatly" will personalize the tone of your communication, whether delivered by phone, letter, or email. Telephone the candidate to discuss and agree a time, and then send your letter or email to confirm the arrangement.

IN FOCUS...
PRE-INTERVIEW QUESTIONNAIRES

One of the world's most influential experts on recruitment, Dr. John Sullivan, recommends that managers give candidates a series of questions to answer before an interview to save valuable time and help interviewers find out more about them beforehand. Candidates might be asked about job preferences, career goals, and motivators, for instance, in questionnaires that are sent to them with the interview invitation and returned before the interview. Such questionnaires could be given only to those candidates who are selected for interview, but Sullivan suggests they could also be used to screen out a few applicants from that pool.

Providing the right information

The invitation sent to candidates must detail the date, time, and place the interview will be held. Send a map or a weblink to a map of the area so they can find the venue easily. Also say who will conduct the interview. Let them know if they need to bring passports, work portfolios, or other documents or materials. Provide advice on how to reschedule their interviews if the given time and date are not convenient. Also give names and contact details such as cell phone numbers so they can let you know if they have been delayed on the interview day.

Considering special needs

When inviting candidates to interviews, ask if they have any particular requirements. These could include:
• making the venue easily accessible if a candidate has mobility problems.
• allowing for or providing an interpreter for hearing- or speech-impaired candidates.
• allowing a friend or relative to accompany a candidate to support or help them.
• providing equipment to help sight-impaired candidates read any necessary material.
• offering a break mid-interview.

ISSUING INVITATION LETTERS

FAST TRACK	OFF TRACK
Addressing the communication to the candidate by name	Sending an interview invitation to "Dear Applicant"
Providing contact names and phone numbers for the interview date in case the candidate has an emergency	Offering no way to contact you on the day of the interview if a candidate has a problem
Taking a proactive approach to adapting interview conditions for candidates with special needs	Telling special-needs candidates they will have to experience the same interview conditions as everyone else

Chapter 2

Conducting the interview

The interview is the first opportunity for you to get to know the person behind the résumé, so every element is extremely important. Keep in mind that the interview will also shape the candidate's impression of your organization.

Setting the tone

When you go to a live performance of a play, from the moment the curtain goes up, the scenery, the backdrop, and the background music give you clues as to what you are about to experience. The same is true for your candidates as soon as they arrive for the interview.

TIP

REMOVE DISTRACTIONS

Leave behind communications tools—office telephones, cell phones, and PDAs , such as BlackBerrys—or keep them turned off.

Selecting a venue

If you have chosen a neutral location such as a hotel as an interview venue, it is best to host your interviews in a comparatively formal setting, such as a suite or conference room instead of a lobby or restaurant where too many distractions await. Similarly, if you hold the interviews at your own premises, book a private room or office so your meetings with candidates will be free from distractions such as phone calls and other interruptions. Check in advance that the setting is neat and does not have personal items, such as inappropriate calendars or posters, in view.

Getting to the right place

Make sure your candidates know where they should go on arrival and who they will see for the interview. These basic details will help them begin the process with confidence. Another boost to the candidates' confidence will come when their first contact welcomes them at the meeting point. Then a comfortable, pleasant place to wait for their interview will suggest that your organization runs smoothly and is committed to making sure candidates begin interviews in the most relaxed state possible.

TIP

MAKE THE VENUE ACCESSIBLE

Avoid sending candidates on their own on complicated routes around floors of offices that will look all the same to them. Appoint an escort to guide them.

Meeting the candidate

Bring with you the candidate's résumé and any other relevant material, such as the questions you intend to ask, the job and person specifications, organizational background, and a notepad and pen. When you meet them, offer a warm, professional greeting using their name and provide a glass of water. Some small talk about their journey to the premises is appropriate.

TIP

BE ON TIME

Be punctual. Keeping the candidate waiting without a genuine emergency reflects poorly on your organization.

✔ CHECKLIST **PREPARING FOR A CANDIDATE**

	YES	NO
• Is your meeting place free from distractions and interruptions?	☐	☐
• Is the candidate aware of where they need to go?	☐	☐
• Do the relevant people such as a receptionist or security personnel know the candidate is coming and where they are to be taken?	☐	☐
• Did you bring the candidate's résumé and other relevant materials such as a list of the questions to be asked?	☐	☐
• Are drinking water and cups accessible nearby?	☐	☐
• Do you know how to pronounce the candidates' names?	☐	☐

Choosing the format

The format of the interview provides a framework for its content. Issues to consider include whether the interview should be conducted one-on-one or two-on-one, or if a panel is required. Circumstances may even dictate that the interview takes place on the telephone or by video conferencing.

Interviewing with a panel

To select a candidate for a very senior, highly technical, or otherwise multifaceted position, interviewing by panel may be the most effective option. A clear structure, so the interview flows and each panel member knows what they are responsible for, is essential to a successful panel interview. So is having a lead or primary interviewer to guide the interview's direction. The secondary panelists can offer clarifying questions and provide additional thoughts later. But remember to limit the numbers—more than four panelists may overwhelm and confuse your candidates.

Teaming up

Most first-stage interviews involve one or two interviewers. Asking questions, listening to and recording answers, observing, and then deciding to either hire the candidate or move on to the next stage of selection is a lot for one person. During the interview, two interviewers can alternate between asking questions and taking notes. Later, two sets of observations and insights are likely to be more helpful toward building a complete picture of a candidate's suitability for a role.

Interviewing at a distance

Distance may make a face-to-face interview impractical. If telephone manner and customer service are significant parts of the job, it would make sense to have a first interview by phone. If you can use a video linkup, the interview will be much the same to conduct as if it was in person. If interviewing by telephone, speak distinctly and keep in mind that it will be even more important to convey warmth and professionalism in your voice. Try smiling naturally as you speak, so it can be heard in your voice and choose a quiet place away from distractions and interruptions.

TIP

TEST THE TECHNOLOGY

Leave time to check that the video-conferencing equipment is working before you begin an interview. If it fails, you will waste time tracking down a technician to make it work.

ASK YOURSELF... HOW SHOULD I CHOOSE AN INTERVIEW FORMAT?

- How complex is the job role?
- At what stage do we need to see the candidate in person?
- What resources are available to conduct an effective distance interview?
- Who else from my organization should be involved in the interviews?
- What will I look to a fellow interviewer to deliver?
- How would we structure a panel interview?

Competency-based questions

The goal of the interviewing process is to find the right candidate who will bring the right skills to the job. Asking candidates to explain how and when they have used the precise competencies in past experiences and situations will give you insight as to their suitability for the job.

Understanding competency

The idea behind competency-based questions is to link past behavior and experiences with the skills needed for the job and future performance. These questions are also known as behavioral questions. Instead of asking what a person would do in a given situation, the interviewer asks candidates to describe how they have handled such a situation previously. This kind of questioning is seen by many professionals as the most reliable because past performance is the best predictor of how a person will perform in the future.

Using the STAR method

The STAR method can guide you through the dual responsibilities of preparing competency questions, and then listening effectively to candidates' responses. STAR is an acronym that stands for Situation, Task, Action, Response. First, outline the type of situation you want the candidates to refer back to in your questions. When a candidate responds, you are listening for a description of a situation that matches the requirements you outlined in the question, a logical approach to solving the problem, specific actions taken to address the challenge, as well as clear results.

"Describe a situation in which you worked with another department."

"Give an example of a time when you had to work with a difficult customer."

"Tell me how you handled a situation in which you had to make a quick decision without having all of the facts."

"Tell me about a time when you had to motivate your team under difficult circumstances."

Assessing competency

"Give an example of how you managed a particularly demanding project."

"This job requires 10 days of travel each month. Please describe the travel requirements of a previous job, and how you dealt with the challenges."

"Please give an example of how you dealt with interpersonal conflict in your team."

"Describe a situation in which you handled conflicting requests from senior managers."

Asking further questions

A clear picture of each candidate's experience and background should emerge from interviews. While competency-based questions should deliver most of the "meat" from your interviews, you will want to obtain information from candidates that may require other types of questions.

VALUE TIME
While asking verification questions, be careful not to waste valuable interview time by asking candidates to recite their résumés to you word for word.

Verifying credentials

Exploring the credentials and past experience that candidates have cited on their résumés is an important part of interviewing. Basic verification questions would cover factual aspects of their education and experience, such as "How long did you attend that college?" and "Which courses did you take?" To obtain more value-based information about their education or experience, ask questions such as: "What motivated you to seek higher education?" and "How did you juggle schoolwork with holding down a part-time job?" Verification questions allow you to check for gaps that could tip you off to an untruth or exaggeration in their list of credentials.

ENCOURAGE STORYTELLING
To ensure fairness, you will be asking each of the candidates the same questions, but prepare to ask follow-up questions to clarify candidates' responses or prompt greater detail.

Diversifying your approach

Open questions, such as "Tell me about yourself," give your candidates a chance to list their skills and experiences to the requirements of the job. If you are seeking factual information, a closed question will be appropriate, for example, "How many staff did you manage?" Probing questions could also be described as follow-on questions because they are likely to follow a response and are intended to encourage the candidate to explain their answer in detail. Unorthodox or unusual questions may prompt intriguing answers, but be certain you know what you want to achieve by asking such a question that, on the surface, has little to do with the job at hand. Questions such as "What is your favorite movie and why?" can inject a light moment into an interview, or they can offer some insight into a candidate's passions and creativity. Stress questions, on the other hand, are designed to reveal how a candidate reacts to pressurized questions. However, introducing added stress into an already stressful interview may be counterproductive!

USING DIFFERENT TYPES OF QUESTIONS

QUESTION TYPE	EXAMPLE	IMPACT
Open	"Tell us about yourself."	Allows candidates to match skills or experiences to the job
Closed	"How many new offices have you opened?"	Secures a brief, specific answer
Hypothetical/ situational	"What would you do if…"	Assesses how candidates think on their feet and gives insight into their priorities and judgment
Probing	"Could you elaborate on how you achieved that result under those circumstances?"	Follow-on questions that are intended to draw out more information
Verification	"Can you confirm when and where you completed your Red Cross CPR Training Course?"	Similar to a closed question; seeking brief answers to verify and confirm factual information
Leading	"Part of the job is publishing a monthly newsletter. Have you done this before?"	Intended to secure a "yes" or "no" answer with more elaboration by the candidate
Stress	"If you were on a plane that was going to crash, who would you save—yourself, your boss, or your mother?"	An aggressive form of questioning that puts the candidate under stress to see how they will react
Unusual/quirky	"If you were a vegetable, what would you want to be and why?"	Aimed at eliciting information about a candidate's creativity and how they think

Respecting diversity

Having a diverse workforce begins with recruiting men and women of different races, religions, nationalities, ages, and sexual orientation into the organization. The interview is the first step to achieving this.

Attracting diversity

To attract the widest variety of employees possible, reflect the presence of diversity in your organization in all of your online and print recruitment materials. Improving interviewing skills is important to finding the right person—but it is also important to remember that the successful candidate can either be a man or a woman and come from varied backgrounds, age groups, lifestyles, and life situations.

EMPLOYEE ASSOCIATIONS
Be aware of employee associations that your organization sponsors for members of different ethnic groups or religions, or if it supports special interest groups.

Recognizing differences

If your candidate pool is diverse, cultural awareness will be essential during your interviews—both to understand how candidates present themselves and how you respond. A smile and a pleasant manner go a long way toward bridging cultural gaps anywhere around the world. Make sure that your interview protocol reflects a positive attitude toward diversity—from your welcome, to the questions you ask, and your body language.

CORPORATE DRESSING
Check if your organization's policy on corporate dress or grooming allows adaptation for different religious requirements for both men and women.

Addressing candidates' cultural concerns

GESTURES AND EYE CONTACT
Understand that a handshake may not be appropriate between men and women, and extended eye contact can signify anger in some cultures.

RELIGIOUS FACILITIES
Find out if there are facilities on site for prayer or rituals during the day, and check the organization's policy regarding time off during religious observances.

EATING HABITS
See if the cafeteria offers vegetarian, kosher, and halal dishes, and if office refrigerators have separate shelves for vegetarian and meat dishes.

Avoiding illegal questions

You may want to ask certain questions to be sure a candidate is the right choice for your organization. As you see it, you are probing the candidate's suitability for the job. But recognize that many questions may be not only inappropriate, but also illegal.

TIP

CONCENTRATE ON JOB-RELATED QUESTIONS
Focus on potential recruits' past achievements, future ambitions, motivations, and what they can bring to your workplace.

Understanding the playing field

Laws vary from country to country regarding which questions are illegal to ask job applicants, and who can or can't work in a country. To avoid legal difficulties, consult your organization's employment law adviser. You might find it difficult to assess what is appropriate to ask candidates, but one rule of thumb is that if the question you want to ask refers to a candidate's personal life and not specifically to a job requirement, it is likely to be illegal to ask.

Asking the right question

Think about what you really want to know about when you consider asking personal questions such as "Which country are you from?"; "Are you planning to have children?"; "What religion are you?"; or "How old are you?" If you believe a candidate's national origin is important, what you probably need to know is, "Do you have a legal right to work in this country?" Your interest in a candidate's family plans may reflect your need to know if they are willing to travel, as the job requires. Instead of asking about a candidate's religion, the relevant issue may be whether they are willing to work particular hours and days of the week. Rather than asking about a candidate's age, pinpoint the issue at the root of the question; is the person physically capable of carrying a certain amount of weight necessary for the job?

Avoiding a wrong move

Using the interview to develop a personal relationship with a candidate is out of bounds. In show business, the phrase "the casting couch" refers to the practice of turning auditions, or interviews, into opportunities to leverage relationships with performers or with authority figures. Business has also suffered from the occasional scandal when a gatekeeper*, such as an interviewer, initiates or accepts inappropriate overtures. During the interview, you and the candidate may discover a common interest that both of you wish to pursue outside the business environment. However, pursuing a relationship—no matter how innocent—as a result of the interview could lead your organization's management to question your judgment on candidate selection. It could also lead to legal and reputation difficulties for you and your organization. Avoid at all costs.

*****Gatekeeper**—*a person who controls access of people, commodities, or information to an organization or to the public.*

NAVIGATING LEGAL ISSUES

FAST TRACK	OFF TRACK
Asking which languages they know	Asking where they were born
Asking if they are willing to relocate	Asking if they are married
Asking if they would be able to perform all the job responsibilities	Asking if their religion allows them to do a certain type of work
Asking if they belong to any professional associations that are relevant to the job	Asking which kinds of social, religious, or political groups they belong to
Offering a glass of water before and during the interview	Inviting them out for a coffee on a personal basis

Effective observation

The point of the interview is to gather as much information as possible about the candidates who have applied for a particular job. To obtain this information, you must ask questions and then listen carefully to the answers. Visual observation of the candidates is also important.

TIP

BE PATIENT
Fight the urge to interrupt or finish interviewees' sentences; be comfortable with a certain amount of silence before moving on to the next point.

Listening actively

Focus on what the candidate is saying, by both listening to the words and observing changing vocal tone, volume, and pace. If you are taking notes, listen for key ideas from the candidate's answer— don't try to write down every word they say. When the candidate has finished responding, make sure you have understood by summarizing one or two of the key points back to them. Then gather more information by asking the candidate to clarify or elaborate their response.

Communicating nonverbally

Your nonverbal cues can either reinforce or contradict the interview's stated purpose. For example, encouraging a candidate verbally to "Tell me about yourself" while fiddling with a paper clip sends conflicting messages. Sitting back in your chair with arms folded can be taken to mean that you are skeptical of what they are saying, and suggest a closed mind, even if that is not how you actually feel. Checking your watch can be interpreted as a desire for the meeting to be over. On the other hand, leaning forward as the candidate speaks, maintaining eye contact, smiling, and occasionally nodding to acknowledge that you are taking on board what they are saying, lets interviewees know you are engaged.

Nonverbal clues

When you observe the candidate during the interview, you too are looking for signs of engagement. The ability to listen and an interest in the job in question are among the first requirements. Also look for nonverbal clues to character, ability to interact with others, confidence, and other traits that would affect a candidate's future success in the job. Physical gestures such as head nods and hand movements can suggest interest in a conversation or a particular topic. Other body movements, such as finger or foot tapping or leg swinging can reflect discomfort, perhaps boredom, or tension. Inappropriate laughter can be a sign of nerves. Be sure to write down what you observe.

Concluding the interview

You have explored your candidate's résumé, explained the job and person specification, and gained insight into the skills and knowledge they would bring to the job. Now it is time to end the meeting. Bringing the interview to a successful close will help both candidate and interviewer move seamlessly into the next stage of the recruitment process.

TIP

GAUGE INTEREST
After the interview, gauge a candidate's interest in the role by their enthusiasm and the eagerness they show in any follow-up.

Questioning the interviewer

When you have finished asking the questions, ask the candidate to offer any additional information they have not covered that is relevant to the job. Also invite them to ask any questions they have. Be prepared to answer questions about the impact of current events on your organization. If your organization has been in the news recently, candidates may want to ask you about the issues involved. The candidate who has researched your organization before the interview should know what your organization does, but you should be ready to answer any questions they may have about the organization's plans for growth, diversification, or consolidation, and how the job on offer fits into a long-term strategy. This stage may well be too early to discuss salary and benefits, but come prepared to respond to such a question, even if it is only to say, "We will discuss those points at a later date." After they have asked their questions, ask the candidates if the job still interests them and whether they would like to proceed to the next stage.

IN FOCUS...
KEEPING THE END MOVING

Be alert to signs that the candidate suspects the interview has not gone well, and that they are going to try to make up for any miscommunication in the last few minutes of the interview. If a candidate wants to return to a particular response to one of your questions or clarify a point, you could gain additional insight that will be helpful to your decision. However, letting them overexplain with no real point is helpful to no one. Know when it's time to cut the chat short.

Moving forward

The candidate will also want to know what will happen next. Be as open and clear as possible about the process ahead. If you plan to hire someone based on the first round of interviews, say so. If you will be conducting second interviews, skills tests, or an assessment center, tell them. If you are basing your choice purely on the interviews, let them know the date by which you expect to have made a decision. Likewise, if you plan second-stage meetings, provide the candidate with as much information as possible about when they will be notified if their application is being taken forward and when the next round of selection will begin. You should also be as open as possible about when they will know if their application has not been successful.

Tying up loose ends

Bringing a job interview to a close should leave both parties feeling that the meeting fulfilled their goals; the candidates should feel they have successfully communicated to you their suitability for the role, or alternatively that the role is not right for them. As the interviewer, you should feel you have obtained all the information needed at the current stage of the recruitment process. You should also feel you have a good idea of whether the candidate matches the job and person specifications closely enough to progress to the next selection round. Housekeeping details that require attending to at the end include ensuring that the address, email, and phone number you have on file for the candidate will remain current through the next stage of the selection process. Thank them for coming, and offer a smile and a handshake—if appropriate—to end the meeting.

HOW TO... END THE INTERVIEW

Complete your interview questions.

↓

Invite the candidate to cover ground you missed.

↓

Encourage the candidate to ask questions related to the job.

↓

Confirm the candidate's contact details.

↓

Ask about the candidate's notice period.

↓

Explain what happens next.

↓

Thank the candidate for coming.

Chapter 3

Supplementing the interview

An interview may not be enough to fully gauge your shortlisted candidates' capabilities, on-the-job potential, and suitability for a particular role. Even after an in-depth interview, you will need the help of additional tools to find out more about the candidate.

Gathering further information

No matter how well planned, the basic interview does not guarantee a complete picture will emerge of how well a candidate fits all the requirements of a given role. Background information is required, and you may have to get help from professionals to make the right decision.

TIP

KNOW THE LEGAL REQUIREMENTS
Some jobs may have mandatory minimum qualifications prescribed by law. Make sure you are aware of any requirements for the job on offer.

Uncovering skills

Résumés and interviews are vehicles for candidates to "tell" what they can do and what they have done. However, they don't allow them to actually "show" their aptitude for certain competencies required. Nor do they let candidates demonstrate how they would perform in a typical work scenario. In jobs requiring high levels of skill, for example, it may be necessary to verify that candidates actually have the required specialized skills. Depending on the job's complexity, various kinds of tests and activities can be conducted to uncover a candidate's professional skills, ability, and aptitude.

Establishing background

In some cases, the sensitive nature of some job roles, such as working with children or hazardous chemicals, may need examination of the candidates' background to confirm they are suitable for that role. As new technology offers opportunities to investigate the ways in which people put themselves forward to friends, family, and colleagues, you can now take other steps to make sure candidates are a good organizational fit.

Using professional assessment

TIP

Expert assistance will probably be required to help you conduct most of the in-depth assessments to make sure you select the best person for the job. Ask your HR director to recommend assessment professionals. You can even consult psychologists and test publishers. But regardless of your consultant's knowledge, it is your responsibility to understand what information you need to know about each candidate—this will arm your experts with the knowledge they need to create the most effective tools in obtaining this information.

PLAN YOUR STRATEGY

Work with your expert consultants to decide the supplemental assessments needed before you advertise the role. Then you can advise candidates about the breadth of the selection process.

ASK YOURSELF... WHAT MORE DO I NEED TO KNOW?

- Are there specific personal characteristics that are needed in the job?
- Which hard competencies are required, for example, typing, standard office software, numeracy, proficiency in a foreign language, or data checking?
- How well would the candidate interact with clients or deliver a presentation?
- Will I want to verify past employment, qualifications, or, in some cases, immigration status and right to work in the country?
- Does the job require working with vulnerable people, such as children?
- How do the candidates represent themselves to professional and personal peers?

Holding an assessment center

To test for job-specific skills, capabilities, and personal traits, you may want to hold an assessment center. The term "assessment center" doesn't refer to a specific place. It is a series of exercises designed to reveal candidates' personal characteristics, capabilities, skills, and potential to succeed in the job you are hiring for.

TIP

INCLUDE A SOCIAL EVENT

Hosting a reception or lunch for your candidates will allow you to see how they respond to others away from the assessment environment.

Matching tests and roles

The assessment center is your opportunity to scrutinize candidates against the selection criteria you outlined in the job description and person specification. In addition to measuring job skills, an assessment center also requires that candidates adapt to a variety of different challenges under the watchful eyes of qualified assessors who observe their behavior while they perform tasks and participate in activities. The nature of the exercises and activities included will depend on the type of job to be filled and should require candidates to demonstrate the skills and abilities they would actually need on the job.

TIP

GIVE FEEDBACK

Be sure feedback on performance is offered to all participants. They need to know which traits or skills the assessments highlighted as meeting or not meeting the job requirements.

Planning exercises

At a typical assessment center, exercises might include: online or paper-and-pencil tests to assess personality, aptitude, and skills; in-tray exercises based on day-to-day work situations; interviews; role-play and simulation scenarios; presentations; and group activities. For more senior and complex roles, the exercises may take several days. The event could be held at your organization's head office or a neutral location, such as a hotel, leased office space, or convention center. Consider how many candidates must attend when deciding how much space will be needed.

Standardizing tests

Creating an assessment center requires the involvement of experts to design the exercises and assess candidates. Expert advice and analysis are critically important when you want to use psychological testing in your selection process. The International Task Force on Assessment Center Guidelines underscores that training assessors is crucial to an effective assessment center. It recommends that when you are choosing assessors, take into account their knowledge and experience with similar assessment techniques, plus their familiarity with the organization and the job to be filled. You may want to train people from within your own organization as assessors, but you could also consider using professional psychologists.

HOW TO... PLAN AND RUN AN ASSESSMENT CENTER

Conduct an analysis to pinpoint the behaviors, competencies, and characteristics necessary for the job.

↓

Deploy a variety of appropriate assessment techniques.

↓

Appoint a number of assessors to observe and evaluate each candidate.

↓

Train assessors thoroughly.

↓

Put in place a system to record candidates' performance accurately.

↓

Pool relevant information afterward.

IN FOCUS... HISTORY OF MILITARY ASSESSMENT CENTERS

The purpose of assessment centers is to give an idea of how a candidate operates in a work situation. They were first used by the military to aid in the selection of officers. The German military used job simulations, along with other capability measurements, to select officers after World War I. The US Office of Strategic Services ran a three-day program of tests to improve its spy selection during World War II. In each case, the intention was to discover how candidates responded to the pressures of real-life situations. Starting in 1942, the British War Office adopted its own system for selecting officers loosely based on observations of the German method.

Using psychometric tests

Organizations increasingly use psychometric tests to help identify in individuals the specific characteristics, abilities, and aptitudes that are likely to predict a person's success in a particular job.

Understanding psychometrics

Psychometric tests measure psychological variables, such as intelligence, aptitude, and personality traits, and are available from credible psychometrics providers. They often involve answering multiple-choice questions, and many can be administered both offline and online. Sometimes these assessments are used to develop psychological profiles of candidates, covering personality and intellectual ability. They can also be used to measure emotional intelligence, preferred work style, candidates' ability to learn, and their potential to achieve in the future. An example of a psychometric instrument is the Myers-Briggs Type Indicator. With this tool, users' responses to a series of multiple-choice questions determine which of 16 personality types they most closely match.

CONFIDENTIALITY
Only people with a legitimate "need to know" as part of the selection process should have access to results.

Choosing what to measure

A thorough study of the manual that comes with each test will help you understand the research that has been conducted to assure that particular assessment's effectiveness. Statistical information outlining its reliability, predictability, and other factors can help you decide if a particular test is right for helping you find out what you want to know.

STANDARDIZATION
The tests must be given under controlled conditions and scored using standard criteria.

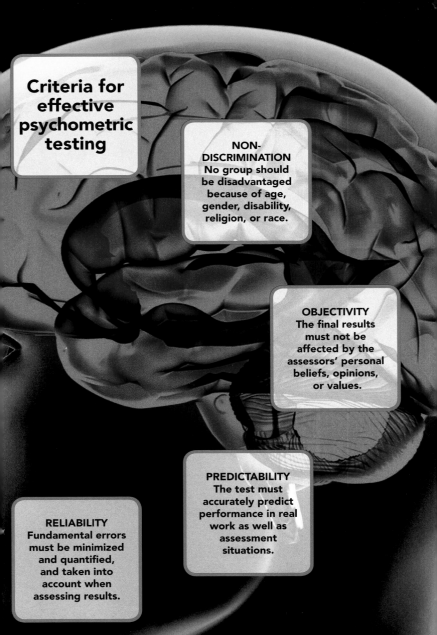

Criteria for effective psychometric testing

NON-DISCRIMINATION
No group should be disadvantaged because of age, gender, disability, religion, or race.

OBJECTIVITY
The final results must not be affected by the assessors' personal beliefs, opinions, or values.

PREDICTABILITY
The test must accurately predict performance in real work as well as assessment situations.

RELIABILITY
Fundamental errors must be minimized and quantified, and taken into account when assessing results.

Testing skills and ability

Depending on the kind of job you're recruiting for, tests that measure certain types of learned knowledge and skills may be very useful to the selection process. Tests are available to assess your candidates' abilities and aptitudes in many areas, from IT skills to spatial reasoning*.

*Spatial reasoning —the ability to visualize images, mentally move them around, and understand how their positions change with movement in one direction or another.

Testing professional skills

How do you know if candidates can do what they say they can do? With certain types of professional skills, it is easy and cost effective to find out by testing for them. Today, it is possible to measure many skills using web-based tests, and it is possible to give candidates a choice as to where they take the tests, For example, a specified location, such as during an on-site assessment center, at their home, or wherever there is access to the Internet.

A skill-testing service will be able to provide you with a myriad of tests that gauge proficiency in specific IT disciplines, foreign languages, administrative operations, such as credit management, payroll and office software, industrial specialties, and virtually every kind of job in business that involves processes, technical knowledge, or data usage. Expect test scores to be accompanied by a report that analyzes the results, so those making the hiring selection can understand candidates' individual strengths and weaknesses in depth.

Q IN FOCUS...
ABILITY VS APTITUDE

The terms "ability" and "aptitude" are often used interchangeably, but various tests may differentiate between the two. Ability might be defined as an enabling proficiency, which means someone can do a particular thing, often thanks to a learned skill or qualification. Aptitude reflects more a candidate's capacity or talent to do something. Some view "ability" as the basis of aptitude, and aptitude as more job-related than ability. Another way of looking at it is to think of ability as a person's capability to do something, and aptitude as the potential to become capable of doing it.

Measuring aptitude and ability

Aptitude is more about a person's propensity for a particular type of thinking or reasoning, which is necessary to succeed in the role, than it is about a well-developed skill. For example, an individual who understands the relationship between shapes, dimensions, and space could be said to have an aptitude for spatial reasoning, the focus of some specialized aptitude tests. Abstract reasoning, or the ability to analyze information and solve problems, is another common theme of aptitude testing. Aptitude for a given discipline can be very important, particularly when hiring for jobs in which you expect the successful candidates to undergo future training to become qualified or proficient at the job.

In some cases, instead of measuring aptitude, you may need to get an idea of candidates' abilities to communicate and use basic arithmetic. A verbal ability test would typically cover word usage, spelling, different parts of speech, reading, and following instructions. Multiplication, division, and reading charts and graphs might be included in a numeric ability test.

CREATE YOUR OWN TESTS

Explore the possibility of building your own tests. Some test suppliers offer this option, depending on the job and the skills you want tested.

CHOOSING APPROPRIATE TESTS

FAST TRACK	OFF TRACK
Defining which abilities and skills are needed for the job	Being unaware or doubtful about which abilities and skills are needed
Seeking out tests that will measure those skills and abilities	Believing all candidates when they say they can meet all requirements
Scrutinizing the analytical reports, which should accompany the test	Considering only the overall scores on the tests

Conducting group activities

Role play and group activities offer great benefits when they are used as part of the recruitment process. Unlike psychometric and aptitude tests, these exercises give candidates a chance to put their interpersonal skills center stage and put theory into practice.

TIP

PRACTICE DISCRETION

Do take notes during group activities. Take a discreet approach so as not to make participants feel you are waiting for them to make a mistake.

Watching candidates in action

You've been getting some insight into your candidates' aptitude and personality traits—now you will see them put their skills, experience, social abilities, and work habits to use in simulated workplace events. This is where you and your assessors will have to work your hardest to observe and record actions and responses. This blend of verbal communications and body language should fill in many of the remaining blanks about your candidates, for example, their ability to work in a team, how well they think in stressful conditions, and whether they are effective listeners. Although cultural differences may affect a person's nonverbal behavior, you can often glean hints about someone's attitudes by observing basic facial expressions and body language.

Planning activities

Keep the rules simple and clear. Specific time allowances must be met, the target goal of a team project must be defined, the guidelines for giving a presentation must be outlined, and the characters and scenarios to be portrayed in role-play events must be understood by the participants. The exercises must be planned well and pose genuine challenges to the participants. However, their structures must not be so complicated that participants are confused instead of stimulated.

Reading basic body language

LEANING FORWARD
Implies the person is interested in what is being said, especially if the head is also held forward.

FIDGETING
Might reflect nervousness. Examples include constantly adjusting one's clothes, or toying with nearby objects.

CROSSING ARMS OR LEGS
Can suggest defensiveness to people or the situation, but can also mean the person is feeling cold.

EYE ROLLING
Might indicate frustration, annoyance, or contempt for another person's opinion or action, even if it is done silently.

DRUMMING OR TAPPING FINGERS
Could signify a person's agitation, boredom, or impatience in a given situation.

MAINTAINING EYE CONTACT
Can mean interest in what is being said, while a fixed stare can mean the person is feigning interest.

Structuring the exercises

Do you want your role-play exercises to involve only your job candidates? Or do you want at least one of the roles taken on by a player who is not involved? Remember: the more candidates you involve in the exercise, the more qualified observers you will need on hand to ensure each job applicant is carefully and equally assessed. Sometimes assessment center organizers bring in actors who are skilled in dramatic improvisation to portray other characters in role-play exercises so observers can focus their attention on the candidates. Bringing in additional experts will boost the cost of your assessment center, which may already be expensive. However, the importance of getting the right person for the particular role or roles you are hiring for could justify the extra cost. An actor could also facilitate a chaired discussion, unless you would like to put a candidate in the role of chair. Putting one candidate in the role of chair can be an effective tool to assess that person's ability to facilitate a group discussion or project. However, that could lead to the participants getting an impression that the person portraying the chair is the favored candidate to get the job. Rotating candidates in and out of the chair's role may draw better performance from the group as a whole.

✔ CHECKLIST **PREPARING FOR GROUP ACTIVITIES**

	YES	NO
• Have you ordered the right activity materials?	☐	☐
• Will the space accommodate the activities you have planned?	☐	☐
• Will you have enough assessors to observe candidates effectively?	☐	☐
• Have you structured the activities clearly with goals and allotted completion times?	☐	☐
• Do the assessors know what you are looking for from each exercise?	☐	☐

CHOOSING ROLE PLAY AND GROUP ACTIVITIES

ACTIVITY	HOW IT WORKS	WHAT IT REVEALS
Leaderless discussion	Candidates are given a problem to discuss for a specific length of time, during which they must develop solutions.	Leadership, negotiation, influencing, and verbal communication skills, creativity, and nonverbal communication style
Practical task	This is a creative problem-solving exercise, which may involve constructing an object with unusual materials or by moving them around in an unusual way.	Interpersonal, teamwork, project management, and problem-solving skills
In-tray or e-tray exercise	Designed to simulate a typical workload for the person who gets the job, the exercise may include memos, budget forecasts, trend information, reports, messages, and emergencies that must be dealt with within a given length of time.	Managerial capabilities such as organization, task prioritization, delegation, time management, and attention to detail while also being able to take a holistic view to solving problems, making decisions, and planning
Oral presentation	Candidates must prepare a talk on a given topic with minimal preparation time.	Creativity, confidence, preparation, ability to think on feet and to structure and effectively communicate a message
Role play	A scenario involving two or more people is created in which a candidate plays a specified role and deals with a specific on-the-job situation.	Communication, listening and negotiation skills, empathy, problem solving, responses to certain situations
Case study	Candidates are briefed on a typical business problem and must make recommendations.	Ability to analyze information and make decisions
Business game	Candidates working in groups compete to come up with the best solution to a business problem, such as a bankruptcy or hostile takeover bid.	Skills in teamwork, creative decision-making, situational analysis

Background screening

Knowing exactly who a candidate is before you bring that person on board will be crucial to your organization's well-being. Issues such as identity, false career information, criminal pasts, and illegal immigration are important and need to be checked early on to avoid problems later.

HOW TO... CHECK OUT NEW EMPLOYEES

Verify their identity.

↓

Verify academic records.

↓

Verify professional credentials.

↓

Check right-to-work documents.

↓

Commission public and criminal records check.

↓

Consider other checks as needed.

Protecting your organization

It is obvious that an organization needs to be certain new employees will bring all of the education, qualifications, skills, and experience they claim to have, in order for the organization to benefit. You want to believe everything candidates have told you on their résumés and in interviews, and trust they have told you everything. But strong competition for particular jobs and tightened employment standards in certain industries mean there is a greater likelihood of candidates falsifying, or omitting necessary information, from their applications. Failing to take steps to confirm candidates' identity and background can leave your organization vulnerable to a number of serious risks such as employee fraud, legal liability and litigation, theft of sensitive organization and customer information, damage to the organization's reputation, and costs stemming from negligent hiring procedures.

Deciding what you need to know

Senior-level roles, certain specialized jobs, and positions giving access to sensitive information or vulnerable people may require more extensive and complex checks of candidates. You may want to outsource complicated screening to a specialized agency. But consider first which checks would be most relevant to the job, organization, and industry involved.

Confirming identity

The most basic vetting procedure is to check references for past schooling, membership in professional organizations, and employment details candidates have given you. However, previous employers may be reluctant to confirm details other than dates of employment because of possible legal action if the candidate does not get the job. Get candidates to help you with simple methods of confirming identity and address by having them bring in identity documents with a photograph (such as a passport or driver's license), a recent bank statement (within the last three months), and a utility bill addressed to them at their current home. Foreign candidates must provide documentation that they are currently eligible to work in your country.

TIP

AVOID DISCRIMINATION
Ask all candidates to show you their passports so you are not singling out non-natives for travel document checks.

Using social networking sites

The Internet is used by many people to share details of their personal lives. Some employers use social networking sites on the Internet as yet another bank of information to check out potential new employees, while others believe such checks invade candidates' privacy.

BE AWARE OF REPUTATION
Type your organization's name into a search engine to check online mentions to find out what employees are saying about your own organization.

Knowing what to look for

Research by job site CareerBuilder.com revealed that in the US, one-third of the hiring managers who screened candidates via social networking profiles reported they dismissed some from consideration after finding inappropriate content. Material regarded as deal-breakers included information about using drugs, badmouthing employers or colleagues, lying about qualifications, criminal behavior, and making discriminatory remarks related to race, gender, or religion. However, 24 percent reported finding content that helped solidify their decision to hire a particular candidate, if, for example, their profile reflected achievement or creativity. To use such sites effectively, you must know what information you are looking for.

CASE STUDY

Enterprise Rent-A-Car
There's no doubt that social networking sites are a major phenomenon, but not all of the world's top employers are inclined to use them—even when an employer is well known as a top employer of graduates, who are generally among the dominant users of such sites. To the accompaniment of considerable news coverage, the European human resources director of international car rental organization Enterprise Rent-A-Car revealed that her recruiters would not research job candidates via social networking sites. According to her, scrutinizing personal web pages invades the candidates' privacy. By using personal web pages for business purposes, employers would be blurring the lines between what is personal and what is business, she told interviewers.

Exploring profiles online

To find out more about a candidate's professional affiliations, contacts, and background online, first type that person's name into your search engine to see if any web mentions come up. If a listing appears, click on the link related to a business-focused social networking site. However, it may ultimately be best simply to avoid social networking sites such as Facebook and MySpace, which focus more on personal life.

Your decision to research candidates on social networking sites must be based on your organization's values. If your organization has a conservative culture, exploring such sites may result in your finding material that turns a previously appealing candidate into a less interesting one. But if your organization has a creative culture, your view of some candidates could be enhanced if their web pages feature an innovative design or information about a meaningful project.

TIP

CHECK YOUR LIABILITY

If you outsource any recruitment to third parties, make sure they follow your policy on using, or not using, social networking sites to check out candidates. Using the sites inappropriately could mean joint liability.

CHECKING SOCIAL NETWORKING SITES

FAST TRACK	OFF TRACK
Visiting professionally focused sites	Visiting sites used primarily for socializing with friends and family
Considering professional references on candidates' profiles	Looking for embarrassing photos or video clips
Looking at the online networking groups they belong to	Seeking out personal details, such as a current pregnancy, which does not affect hiring decisions
Studying their public profiles for work-related information	Making inappropriate contact with candidates

Chapter 4

Making the final decision

The information required to make the hiring decision is in your hands, but the difficult task of analyzing and prioritizing the strengths and potential of each candidate still lies ahead—as does the decision of choosing the best person for the role.

Aligning goals

Hiring a new person into your organization is more than simply filling a slot. It is not enough for the new employee to meet today's needs. In this fast-moving world, new employees must be capable of growing and developing along with the organization.

TIP

PREDICT THE BEST DEVELOPERS
Remember that past performance is a strong indicator of future performance. Candidates with a track record of embracing development elsewhere are likely to embrace it at a new job.

Developing tomorrow's team

To position themselves for future success, organizations must understand where they are at the moment and what they must do to reach where they want to go. New skills and new kinds of jobs will be essential to the forward-moving organization. The people who are hired into their midst now must be sufficiently flexible to be effective contributors to the organization of tomorrow. Think about the candidates you are interviewing and choosing between. Who wants to be comfortable and do the same task in the same way, and who seeks a challenge and wants to develop?

Matching values

In some cases, you may be hiring a person specifically to lead the way toward development and growth. Consider your organization's other goals and values—how do you want to move ahead, and are there right and wrong ways to accomplish this? While it is important to allow and encourage creative differences when examining different options offered by candidates, bear in mind that bringing in a person with fundamentally different values could result in a costly mistake that sets your organization back.

TIP

SUPPORT DURING CHANGE

Sometimes a change in values is necessary for an organization. If this is true in yours, you must openly endorse and back the new employee's moves to make changes happen in spite of organizational inertia.

Defining the right matches

Draw up a document that outlines your organization's strategic goals and defines the behaviors, skills, and abilities that would support them. Take the exercise further by outlining the strategic goals of the team for which you are hiring, and define the attributes, experience, and abilities that would help them achieve these goals. This approach will require you to understand the direction of both the organization and the team. Hopefully, the two are complementary. It will usually be easier to define strategic goals for the organization; individual teams may not always outline theirs. Work with them to do so—however, be warned that this requires care and considerable thought. Then when matching up the abilities, attitudes, behaviors, and skills of each of your candidates to the items on the two lists, you will begin to see where alignment and compatibility exist, and where they don't.

ASK YOURSELF... WHAT DO WE NEED TOMORROW?

- What does your organization want its unique selling proposition to be in five years' time?
- What new skills will you need to accomplish that?
- How must our organization develop to fulfill its long-term goal?
- What are the requirements needed by today's manager to lead the organization to achieve that goal?
- How do the above needs relate to the position you are filling now?

Assessing strengths

It is rare that a candidate offers all the required attitudes, characteristics, skills, and experience to succeed in the role in question. Adopting a methodical approach to weighing up and comparing candidates' qualities is the key to deciding which blend of strengths is best for the job.

Using the framework

At the beginning of the recruitment process, you drew up job and person descriptions to set out the demands of the role and the experience, character, and qualifications required. You may also have created a decision matrix to give these requirements some sort of priority. When you reach the stage of making a final decision, return to these documents and use them as a framework against which to review the information gathered from interviews, tests, assessment center activities, and résumés.

Weighting responses

Ask yourself what percentage of your hiring decision will be based on information gained in the interview itself—100 percent, 50 percent, or less? If the decision will depend primarily, or entirely, on the interviews, then devise a weighting system for the responses to each question. Let's say that you decide each answer would be worth a maximum of five points. At the same time, each question would have a different value depending on its importance to the hiring decision. For example, a candidate might earn four points for the quality of her response to a question, which has a weighted value of three points. The total earned value of her response to that question would be 12 points (4 x 3).

Scoring strengths

If you held an assessment center, bring into the hiring equation the information obtained through the psychometric tests, exercises, and other activities. Create a score sheet or assessment sheet for each candidate. List each element or activity you "tested" or "scored" them on, and take note of the appropriate score, points, or place on the behavioral spectrum*. Or you could keep it simples and put a check by the elements where they performed to an acceptable level and double checks for outstanding performance. What kind of picture is emerging of each of the candidates? Is there one candidate who clearly stands out from the rest? Or are there several with a similar collection of strengths? Eliminate the most obviously weak performers among your candidates. Discuss with your colleagues and any external experts the strengths demonstrated by the candidates who remain contenders, and ascertain if they are the most critical strengths needed by the organization.

*Behavioral spectrum—*the full range of behaviors a person may exhibit or actions they might take during an assessment center activity.*

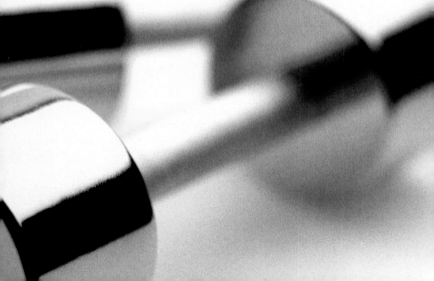

CONSIDER ANY ORGANIZATIONAL CHANGES

Take into account any changes that have occurred in your organization since recruitment began. It may be necessary to reconsider candidates' strengths in light of new priorities.

Linking goals

Next, consider the organization and team goals you identified, along with the list of abilities, behaviors, and skills required to support them. Compare these with the strengths of each individual candidate as outlined on the score sheet. Ideally, the candidate whose skills, experience, and other characteristics most closely meet the job criteria will also be shown to be a good fit with the organization and team goals. Remember throughout the selection process that you are measuring candidates against the required criteria, and not comparing them to fellow candidates. Being human, it is inevitable that some discussion will result in candidate comparison, but keep in mind that you are looking for the best match to the job and to the organization.

HOW TO...
MAKE YOUR DECISION

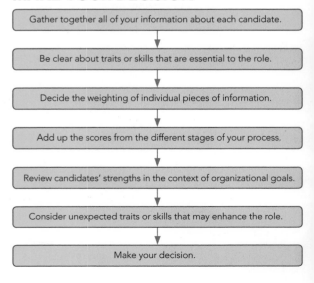

Gather together all of your information about each candidate.

Be clear about traits or skills that are essential to the role.

Decide the weighting of individual pieces of information.

Add up the scores from the different stages of your process.

Review candidates' strengths in the context of organizational goals.

Consider unexpected traits or skills that may enhance the role.

Make your decision.

Experiencing a surprise

As you approach your decision, remember that a methodical approach to hiring is the best way to make sure the job criteria, person specification, and organization goals are given due consideration when choosing candidates. However, keep your mind open to the unexpected if a candidate has demonstrated an unanticipated skill, personality trait, or other quality that adds a new dimension to their application for the job. Perhaps the candidate lacks a qualification, trait, or experience you initially considered essential for the role but offers something else that you had not thought about, in spite of your in-depth examination of the job requirements. If you are seriously considering this candidate, consider whether you can make that trade-off without it having a negative effect somewhere along the line. But also be clear about which characteristics, skills, or experience you cannot afford to do without. Traits such as integrity and a constructive, positive management style should be nonnegotiable, and a specific qualification may be less important to your organization than a candidate's unexpected expertise in a new and exciting technology.

TIP

MAKE THE MOST OF UNEXPECTED SKILLS

When a candidate has an unanticipated skill that could be valuable to the organization, think about whether it is needed now or if a new role should be created to incorporate it.

ASK YOURSELF... WHAT ARE THE CRITICAL UNKNOWNS?

- How well will the candidate work in a team?
- How do they respond to stress?
- What is their management style?
- What motivates them to perform?
- How well will their personality mesh with their potential manager?
- How flexible and adaptable are they to new conditions?
- How well do they think on their feet?
- Are they problem solvers?
- Do they have an unexpected skill or ability that may enhance the role?

Making the offer

The process does not end once you have chosen a candidate. The next stage involves creating a job offer for them and inviting them to build a future in your organization.

Building the package

The salary is one of the offer elements that can make or break the deal. Most employers benchmark salary data to make sure they pay their employees competitive wages for their marketplace and offer an attractive selection of benefits. At the least, studying recent salary surveys for jobs in your industry sector will help you to adjust the basic salary you will offer your new employees, to reflect the appropriate levels of education and experience, as well as the geographic region.

Informing the selectees

Once you have put together an offer, telephone your chosen candidate to share the good news verbally before you send out the letter. Mention a few of the offer highlights, such as pay and start date. They may ask for a few days to consider the opportunity after studying the written offer, which is perfectly acceptable. However, an attempt to significantly renegotiate the offered salary should be viewed with caution, particularly if a range was originally advertised.

OTHER DETAILS
Confirm a deadline for accepting the offer, a start date, name of the line manager, and the job location.

WORK HOURS
Outline the typical work hours and days, any flexible working hours, and any probation period.

REFERENCES
Make it clear to the recruits that the offer is contingent upon suitable references.

Making the offer

SALARY AND BONUSES
Be aware of average salary and bonus or commission levels for this role.

BENEFITS
Spell out in detail the benefits, for example, insurance, discounts, and vacation days.

COMPANY ASSETS
Advise which assets come with this role, such as a cell phone, car, or PDA.

Obtaining references

Confirming the selection of your top candidate will depend on obtaining suitable references. You may have explored their professional background and right to work in your country, but taking the additional step of gleaning specific, job-relevant information about your candidate from people who know him or her is crucial to closing the deal.

TIP

EXPAND THE REFERENCE BASE

Consider accepting a reference from a community group or volunteer project who can discuss the person's skills and attributes relevant to the job.

Lining up references

Advise your candidates early in the recruitment process that if you should decide to hire them, you will need the names and contact details of two or three professional references who would be willing to speak to you about their current or previous jobs. Emphasize to candidates that employment will be contingent on your being able to obtain suitable references.

Requesting information

It is not uncommon for hiring managers today to send out forms requesting information on their potential employees, to make it easier for anyone giving a reference to provide information. However, it is best if you can actually speak to someone giving a reference. If you are able to speak with them directly, ask the basics, but also inquire about the quality of the candidate's work, strengths and weaknesses, ability to work with others, and any anecdotes that offer insight into how they made a difference in the workplace. Other questions may come to mind, too, but make sure you ask only work-related questions. Do not inquire about anything you wouldn't be willing to ask the candidate directly, such as issues to do with race, religion, ethnicity, marital status, or age.

Raising questions

Hopefully you will receive information that confirms your best impressions about the person you have selected for the job. However, do make contingency plans in case you get a negative report about your potential employee. If you receive one less-than-favorable report but others that are positive, ask your candidate for another reference you may contact; there may have been a personality conflict between manager and employee, the manager may have been jealous of the employee, or perhaps that particular job was not a good fit for your potential employee. On the other hand, if none seem willing to confirm or verify information the candidate has given you, you may want to reconsider your decision to hire this person. However, sometimes former managers are simply not interested enough to pass on any information, positive or negative, about former employees. This should not be held against the candidate; you will have to consider this a "neutral" reference, and ask the candidate for another. Another scenario that has been known to unfold is the use of family or friends as professional references, so be certain to verify the circumstances in which the person knew the candidate.

TIP

GET IN TOUCH WITH THE INDIVIDUAL GIVING THE REFERENCE

Follow up reference forms and letters with a more direct approach—a phone call—to be sure you get the necessary answers regarding your candidates.

✔ CHECKLIST CREATING A REFERENCE FORM

	YES	NO
• Have you confirmed dates of employment and job title(s) during employment?	☐	☐
• Have you confirmed the candidate's final salary?	☐	☐
• Have you asked about any promotions or honors?	☐	☐
• Have you asked about their responsibilities?	☐	☐
• Can they list the training and development undertaken?	☐	☐
• Can they confirm the candidate's reason for leaving?	☐	☐

Sending rejection letters

Probably the most painful part of recruitment is telling hopeful candidates they did not get the job. They will no doubt share their experiences—good or bad—with their friends or family, so organizations can only gain by treating unsuccessful candidates well.

TIP

TREAT EACH CANDIDATE EQUALLY

Choose your language carefully so no one could build a case for being discriminated against.

Handling with care

Failing to get a job you want is one of life's great disappointments. The bottom line is that you as an individual did not offer everything the employer wanted. Being able to empathize with that blow to self-esteem will go far toward guiding your treatment of the candidates you did not select. Treating them with dignity can create a good impression of your organization as an employer in the marketplace. Even though your attention may be focused on bringing on board your new employee, ensuring those not selected walk away with a positive impression is time well spent.

"We received a number of very strong applications."

"I regret to say your application has not been successful."

"If you have any comments on your experience of our recruitment process, we would be delighted to hear them."

Contacting those who weren't selected

Send all candidates who were not selected a formal letter confirming they did not get the job. The tone must be businesslike, but inject some warmth with a comment referring back to some interesting information the candidate revealed in the interview, if possible. Depending on the number of candidates you interviewed, you may have time to telephone those not selected. If so, tell them they have not been selected, but thank them for applying and wish them well in their job search.

Being positive in your approach

The rejecting letter's main purpose is to tell those who weren't selected they were not successful this time, but it also gives you a vehicle to encourage promising candidates to apply to your organization again. You could also invite them to apply for specific roles in your organization for which they may be better suited. However, letters to the candidates who would not be a good fit for the organization should be just as professional and courteous as those to the people whom you would like to see apply again in the future.

"Thank you for taking the time to come in."

"My colleagues and I greatly enjoyed meeting you."

"We would be happy to consider your application for the more junior position of..."

Reviewing your process

Once you have nearly completed your recruitment process, go back over the steps to examine the results and see where the process could be improved. Your own notes and the opinions of colleagues and experts involved in the process can help with this.

Looking for "red flags"

Analyze your collated data to look for indicators that your process is inadequate. Warning signs might include too few applications from candidates with the right skill sets, or information gaps about candidates' capabilities. Exchange feedback with the colleagues involved in the process about interviewing style, the relevance of questions asked, and what could be improved.

LOCATION
Make sure you place future advertisements in the places where the most appropriate candidates for the role are most likely to see them.

Measuring return on investment

Keep records of the number of days it has taken to hire for the role, from the beginning of the process to the candidate's formal acceptance. Closely monitor the total cost-to-hire—this will include costs incurred for advertising, recruitment consultants, assessment center tests, background checking carried out by external consultants, venue rental, and staff hours. Effectively managing the time it takes to hire means balancing the quick and efficient filling of the position without rushing to put the first available candidate in place. Keeping cost-to-hire at a fiscally responsible level is challenging, and means you must keep an eye on the return-on-investment of each expense.

JOB DESCRIPTION
Ensure future advertisements explain and "sell" the job, and effectively communicate your organization's brand and identity.

Planning your recruitment advertising

MEDIA
Consider which medium—print or online—produced the most candidates, and which specific title or site delivered the best-qualified applicants.

QUALIFICATIONS
Determine whether there was an overabundance or a noticeable lack of certain desired skills/experience offered by candidates.

DIVERSITY
Check whether candidates had similar backgrounds, or they represented the diversity of your customers, clients, and geographic location.

Onboarding new employees

The candidate has been chosen and has accepted your offer. Now it is time to make sure the transition from candidate to employee is seamless. Lay the groundwork for a successful future in the organization by providing the right information and equipment—and a warm welcome.

TIP

PERSONALIZE THE EXPERIENCE

Select a colleague to initiate contact with the newcomer and be a "buddy" during onboarding and induction, to answer questions, and keep the newcomer up-to-date with office projects and activities before they arrive.

Creating a link

If your organization does not already have a program in place for preparing new employees for their new workplace, it is time to build one. One way to start making them feel as though they are already part of the team is to send them employee information, such as a staff handbook, before their first day. Or you could send them a link and log-in for the organization website's intranet so they can get a feel for its day-to-day goings on as well as benefits, social events, dress code, and the organizational structure. If your organization has branded materials, such as pens, T-shirts, or caps, give these items as a gift to communicate the message "You are one of us." If the person is relocating from a distance, send information about the local area, such as accommodation, schools, and leisure facilities.

✔ CHECKLIST BRINGING THE NEWCOMER ON BOARD

	YES	NO
• Have I sent relevant employee information to the newcomer?	☐	☐
• Have I ensured that the line manager or a colleague is prepared for the newcomer's arrival?	☐	☐
• Have I organized a session to explain the team's current projects and how the new employee is expected to contribute to them?	☐	☐

Planning Day One

Advise your new employees where they need to report on their first day, with directions on how to get there. If there is an organization-wide first-day orientation, plan for a colleague from their team to meet them afterward. Then let them spend the first day getting to know the workplace, their work equipment, and their colleagues. A nice touch is for the line manager to take the newcomer out for lunch on the first day to spend some time over a meal discussing the job, plans for the first week at work, and the team's current projects. This can get the relationship off on a good footing by demonstrating the line manager's accessibility to team members.

MAKE THE MOST OF ONBOARDING

Remember that the best onboarding operations involve both technology and the human touch. Technology efficiently takes care of the bureaucracy, such as ordering equipment and passes, and generating necessary paperwork. Humans add a warm welcome.

Mapping the future

Most importantly, your new employee needs to understand your organization's mission, values, and forward strategy. They need to know where they fit in, and how they are expected to contribute to the organization's day-to-day operations as well as the future. Having their job description on hand to review will reinforce their duties and responsibilities. Mapping out a clear idea of the team's targets over the next few months will provide a view of how all the pieces fit together. A well thought-out and welcoming beginning will help newcomers start this phase of their careers with confidence. And that is one of the best ways to retain the best and brightest talent.

IN FOCUS...
ONBOARDING

Top employers now take seriously the need to make joining an organization as smooth and enjoyable a process as possible for its new employees. There is certainly a business case for it, whether applied to an organization's most junior employee or its most senior. Evidence shows that when done well, onboarding promotes productivity, encourages employee retention, and leads to quicker assimilation of newly hired personnel. Well planned onboarding ensures all the necessary paperwork is completed early on, all the necessary work equipment is available from the first day, and that the new job gets off to a running start.

MOTIVATING PEOPLE

Contents

78 Introduction

CHAPTER 1

Creating a motivating environment

80 Supporting performance
82 Principles of motivation
86 Creating the right conditions
88 Creating a high-performance culture
90 Recruiting the right people
92 Measuring motivation

CHAPTER 2

Building processes for motivation

94 Designing a job role
96 Creating a balance
98 Conducting appraisals
100 Setting objectives
104 Measuring progress
106 Training and development
108 Recognizing performance
110 Paying for performance

CHAPTER 3

Developing the skills of motivation

112 Motivating yourself
116 Being a good motivator
118 Making people feel valued
120 Developing communication
122 Identifying demotivation
124 Consulting others
126 Delegating effectively
128 Coaching successfully

CHAPTER 4

Motivating in difficult situations

130 Motivating during change
134 Motivating dispersed workers
136 Motivating underperformers
138 Motivating a project team
140 Motivating teams
142 Bringing it all together

Introduction

Enthusiastic and motivated people are essential for an organization to be successful. A business with motivated staff has an advantage over its competitors. It is easier and quicker for a competitor to copy an idea for a product or service than it is for them to build a motivated workforce.

People now have greater expectations of their employers. They no longer expect to stay with one employer for more than a few years and may even have several different career paths during their working lives. If a skilled worker is unhappy with their employer, they will be able to change jobs without much difficulty. It is often the best people who are able to leave most quickly, making the art of motivation more important than ever.

Motivating People is divided into four sections. The first deals with the essence of motivation: what it is and how you can create the right environment for a motivated team. The second examines the processes you need to underpin and sustain your motivating environment, looking at setting objectives, measuring performance, and at how you reward people. The third teaches you the skills you need to develop in order to motivate your team. The final section looks at motivating in difficult situations such as dealing with change and motivating people who work from home.

Chapter 1

Creating a motivating environment

The context of motivation is important because it is an essential element in the mix that delivers high performance. As a manager you will need to understand the principles of motivation to create the right environment in your organization.

Supporting performance

Motivation is a major driver of individual, team, and organizational success. But having motivated people isn't sufficient to guarantee high performance. There are other factors that must be considered, including having the ability and opportunity to do well.

MOTIVATE EVERYONE

In every team, some members demand more attention than others. Make sure you motivate all team members, even the quiet ones.

Directing efforts

Motivation is the will to do something. It comes from inside us, and herein lies the challenge for management. How do you motivate your people to achieve the organization's goals? Motivation is more than enthusiasm—it is about directing people's efforts. If you are a manager, your performance will depend on the efforts of your employees. Set clear goals for them and keep thinking about how you can support and motivate them. This is essential for the organization's and your own success.

Achieving success

A motivated person or group also requires the opportunity and ability to boost their performance. Opportunity covers two aspects—making sure your people have the tools and resources needed to do the job, and allowing them the space to do the job well without restrictions. A person's ability is a crucial factor that is often overlooked. It is created by combining an individual's innate skill or talent with experience.

? ASK YOURSELF... IS MY TEAM ABLE TO PERFORM?

- Do my team members know what their goals are?
- What aspects of the work and environment demotivate them?
- Which tools are constraining the output?
- Do my team members have the basic ability and training to do their jobs?
- How can I improve the abilities of my team?

Maximizing performance

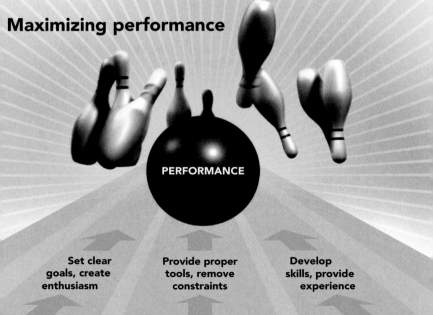

PERFORMANCE

Set clear goals, create enthusiasm

Provide proper tools, remove constraints

Develop skills, provide experience

MOTIVATION

OPPORTUNITY

ABILITY

Principles of motivation

There are three accepted theories of motivation: Maslow's hierarchy of needs; Herzberg's motivation and hygiene factors; and expectancy theory. How you use these, coupled with your own beliefs, will influence how you manage and motivate people.

GET FAMILIAR WITH YOUR STAFF
Remember that everyone is an individual. To motivate someone you need to get to know them well and understand their own personal motivators and demotivators.

Maslow's motivation theory

American psychologist Abraham Maslow, one of the founding fathers of motivation theory, suggested that people have a hierarchy of needs. The basic needs should be satisfied first, and once these are met, you must appeal to the higher level of needs if you are to continue to motivate someone. Maslow's work suggests that people have different needs at different times. Some of these needs will be satisfied at work, and others through life outside work. But if you want to motivate your staff you need to get to know them, their interests, and their aspirations so you can adapt the organization's as well as your own approach to their changing situation.

IN FOCUS... MASLOW'S HIERARCHY OF NEEDS THEORY

Maslow's hierarchy of needs starts with the physiological needs of life: being able to breathe; being fed; and staying warm. The next level is concerned with security: being safe and secure. The third level relates to social needs: love and membership of wider social groups. The fourth level is esteem: the need for respect and a feeling of worth. The final level is self-actualization, where the desire is to be happy through achieving ambitions and fulfilling your potential. Maslow believed that once a lower level need was satisfied, its motivational impact declined and was replaced by higher level needs.

Expectancy theory

Expectancy theory was developed by Professor Victor Vroom in the 1960s. It proposes that people are motivated by being involved in setting their own goals, by receiving feedback along the way, and by recognition for what they achieve. Feedback is important because it is very motivating to know how well you are progressing toward the target.

TIP

LOOK BEYOND SALARY

Focus on the other benefits you can use to motivate people including recognition, advancement, and development.

Herzberg's theory

The psychologist Frederick Herzberg divided sources of motivation into "motivators" and "hygiene factors." Hygiene factors don't motivate, but if they are not dealt with, they can turn people off. Having a dirty office is irritating, but having the cleanest office in the world isn't motivational. Herzberg believed salary is often a hygiene factor. If people are paid fairly, they are satisfied; paying above-average rates doesn't motivate people.

Herzberg's motivators and hygiene factors

MOTIVATION

HERZBERG'S HYGIENE FACTORS

HERZBERG'S MOTIVATORS

Salary	Recognition
Supervision	Progression
Company policy	Achievement
Working conditions	Responsibility
Personal relationships	The work itself

Believing in people

Your beliefs about human nature affect how you manage people. Douglas McGregor, author of *The Human Side of Enterprise*, created two extreme management approaches, which he called theory X and theory Y. Theory X is based on the structuring of work precisely and at a detailed level, directing and controlling what people do, and motivating them through rewards and punishment. Theory Y suggests appealing to people's higher-level needs through communicating and negotiating goals and outcomes. If managers in your organization act as if they believe in theory X, employees are likely to be demotivated. You can set rules to protect the organization from lazy and uncommitted employees.

TIP

UNDERSTAND YOUR STAFF
Be clear about your beliefs on how people behave at work. Keep asking yourself what you can start doing differently each day to keep your staff motivated.

Theory X beliefs
• People are lazy.
• People lack ambition, dislike responsibility, and need to be told what to do.
• People are unconcerned by the organization's goals and need to be driven to perform.

Theory Y beliefs
• Most people are not naturally lazy, and work is a source of satisfaction.
• Most people learn to accept responsibility.
• Most people will work toward objectives to which they are committed.

GIVE CREDIT
Most people appreciate external recognition of their achievements so publicize their success and good work.

OFFER FEEDBACK
Keep talking and discussing with your staff—people need to receive regular feedback on progress in order to continue to perform well.

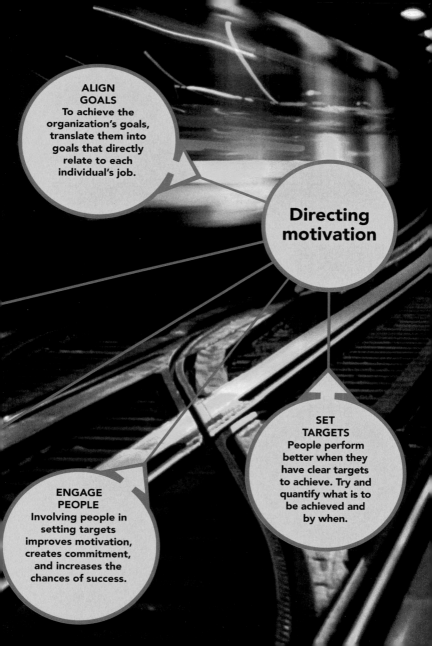

ALIGN GOALS
To achieve the organization's goals, translate them into goals that directly relate to each individual's job.

Directing motivation

SET TARGETS
People perform better when they have clear targets to achieve. Try and quantify what is to be achieved and by when.

ENGAGE PEOPLE
Involving people in setting targets improves motivation, creates commitment, and increases the chances of success.

Creating the right conditions

Broadly speaking, elements of motivation can be divided into two groups: tangible elements, such as the physical working environment, and intangible elements, such as status. Tangible elements are known as "hygiene factors," which are the basic work needs. Intangible elements are known as "motivators." Some, such as pay, straddle both groups. For example, money pays your bills, but higher pay rates can also be a form of recognition.

TIP

KEEP YOUR EARS OPEN

Pay attention to the general office chatter to find out what frustrates people.

Recognizing basic needs

It may seem odd, but working in stylish surroundings is not the greatest motivator. It is very pleasant and can signal a certain status, but it's not essential. The majority of people want to do a good job. They want to work to the best of their ability. It will almost certainly take them longer to do something if they don't have the proper tools to do it. Basic work needs in an average office include:
• Good light and ventilation
• A comfortable temperature
• Sufficient desk space
• A comfortable chair
• Reliable equipment and systems such as a computer, printer, photocopier, and telephone
• An area for refreshment
• A separate area to get away from the desk.

BUILD A REPUTATION

Focus on establishing your organization's credibility—it can take years but will enable you to attract the best employees away from your competitors.

Considering intangible motivators

Intangible motivators are more difficult to identify and usually vary from person to person, although there are some that are common to most people. These fall across a spectrum ranging from those that are fairly easily defined, such as job security, flexible working, recognition, and career development, to those that are very personal, such as achievement—the feeling of having done a job well, belonging to a worthwhile organization, or being part of a well-respected team. These motivators are often highly prized and many people would rather work for an organization of which they are proud, or that takes account of their work-life balance, than for one that simply pays well.

✓ CHECKLIST **ARE WORKING CONDITIONS OPTIMUM?**

	YES	NO
• Is the physical working environment satisfactory?	☐	☐
• Are we offering a reasonable rate of pay?	☐	☐
• Does my team have the right tools for the job?	☐	☐
• Am I aware of what their frustrations are?	☐	☐
• Are we able to offer flexible working hours?	☐	☐
• Are our managers well trained?	☐	☐

Creating a high-performance culture

Some organizational cultures motivate people to perform well, while some motivate people to stay within their job description and not take risks. Your management style will create the culture for your team, so your actions are critical to motivation and performance.

Understanding culture

*Blame culture—
culture in which the
organization tries
to apportion blame
rather than resolve
problems. It is
encapsulated by the
question "Whose
fault is it?"*

Culture is defined by an organization's values and behavior. It is about the way things are done. Supportive cultures create a trusting environment that facilitates motivation. On the other hand, a blame culture* creates a climate of fear. Rather than promoting an environment in which mistakes are not made, it leads to one in which no one will take any risks and where people are more concerned about checking their own work than moving forward and achieving objectives.

CREATING A POSITIVE CULTURE

⬆ FAST TRACK	⊘ OFF TRACK
Demonstrating commitment to the organization's values	Lacking confidence in leaders
Focusing on opportunities	Covering up problems
Creating trust between people	Putting the blame on others
Learning from mistakes	Exercising too much control

Embedding the culture

A culture of openness motivates the whole team to perform. It is created by leaders communicating a clear vision of what they want the values of their organization to be. Many organizations publish their values and display them on their websites and intranet. The organization setting is important, but you should also create your own local team culture. To encourage a culture of openness you will need to respond positively when people present their mistakes or problems. You must use the opportunity to help people learn from their mistakes, rather than pass judgment or criticize their actions. Believing most people want to do a good job will help you do this. Over time, your action will create trust, and people will respond to your approach and confide in you. As you resolve their issues, you will motivate the whole team to perform.

Recruiting the right people

Most managers inherit existing teams and have the task of managing people with a given set of experience, skills, and personalities. When you bring in a new person, you can make a considerable difference to the performance and overall motivation of your team.

Introducing a new employee

Long-established teams usually build good working relationships and have a strong sense of loyalty to the team and the organization, but they can also develop a reluctance to change and make improvements. Individuals may have become bored and be demotivated as a result. Bringing in a person with new ideas can remotivate a team. However, if you bring in the wrong person or handle their integration into the team ineptly, you may damage the team spirit. So it is important to consider a new member carefully.

Finding the right person

There are two key questions to ask when recruiting. The first is: "Does this person have the right experience, knowledge, and skill to do the job?" The second relates to attitude and approach: "How will this person contribute to the team and the organization?" The answers to the first question should be apparent from the individual's résumé, and can be checked at the interview. The answers to the second can be sought during the interview process. Finding out is someone is self-motivated is a challenging task. You can judge whether the individual is self-motivated by ascertaining if they progressed in their previous organization, have learned from mistakes, and if they have interests outside work.

Ensuring successful recruitment

Recruitment is an expensive process, so when you bring in a new person you want to make sure they stay and are successful in improving team performance. Your role as manager is to make sure the new employee has the best start possible. Consider how you will introduce them and integrate them into your existing team. Be sure team members are aware of the person's background and what they will be doing. Brief the individual on their personal objectives and the overall team objectives. If you work in a large organization you may want to appoint a mentor to work closely with the person through the early stages in their new role.

Ⓠ IN FOCUS... DOCTOR BELBIN'S TEAM ROLES

Dr. R. Meredith Belbin, a British researcher and management theorist, established a set of team roles, each associated with a particular type of personality. These included implementers, shapers, completer/finishers, plants (people who have original ideas), evaluators, specialists, coordinators, team workers, and resource investigators (people who explore new ideas). To succeed, teams need a balance of functional ability (the professional skills and technical backgrounds required for the project) and their team roles. Teams work best when there is a balance of roles so that the team members can motivate and learn from each other.

Measuring motivation

Motivation is not something you can easily sense when you walk into an office. You may spot tangible signs, but often they represent just a snapshot of what is happening at a given time. So it is helpful to try to measure the mood of the workforce. This is best done by means of a survey.

TIP

KEEP ASKING FOR FEEDBACK

Persevere with regular surveys, even if the results of the first one shock you. Over time and with attention, you can improve your results and the motivation of your staff.

Conducting a survey

It is generally accepted that motivated employees perform better, so it is important to establish how your employees are feeling as objectively as you can. The best way to get reliable and anonymous feedback about the mood of the workforce is through a regular staff opinion survey. Markus Buckingham and Curt Coffman, management consultants at the Gallup organization, developed a set of 12 questions to measure the motivation of a workforce. Does your staff:

• know what is expected of them at work?
• have the materials and equipment they need to do their job properly?
• have the opportunity to do their best every day?
• receive recognition or praise for good work? Have they in the last week?
• have a supervisor, or someone at work who cares about them as a person?
• have someone who encourages their development?
• believe their opinions at work appear to count?

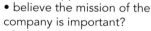

• believe the mission of the company is important?
• believe their coworkers are committed to their work?
• have a best friend at work?
• have someone to talk to about their progress?
• have opportunities at work to learn and grow?

They also suggest you should ask how satisfied your employees are with your organization as an employer. Their research showed responses to the questions can be positively linked to productivity, profitability, customer satisfaction, and staff turnover. Conducting the survey each year will allow you to compare the results over time, and reveal where improvements are being made and where you need to take action.

Providing feedback

If you conduct a survey, it is always important to give feedback. Ideally you should communicate this at team level, but when teams have returned fewer than seven completed surveys, you should not give the results, as anonymity will be undermined. Present and discuss the results openly, focusing on issues raised by the survey and actions that could be taken to prevent problems and improve things in the future. Be careful not to overpromise to keep from creating unrealistic expectations among your employees.

TIP

CHECK THE RESPONSE RATE

When conducting a survey, always measure your response rate—the number responding as a percentage of those sent the survey. A low response in an area can be an early indicator of problems.

MEASURING STAFF OPINION

FAST TRACK	OFF TRACK
Conducting regular staff opinion surveys	Disregarding or being uninterested in staff opinion
Allowing the staff to make their responses anonymous	Discouraging completion of the staff survey
Taking the survey seriously so a majority of staff complete it	Asking the staff ambiguous or irrelevant questions

Chapter 2
Building processes for motivation

Once you have succeeded in creating an environment to develop a motivated workforce, you need to implement and maintain processes to underpin it. These processes provide a structure that demonstrates "how things are done."

Designing a job role

Jobs roles are changing as a result of the breaking down of hierarchy in organizations. Individuals now have a greater choice of what their job profile should be, so to retain the best employees and motivate them at work, you will need to design their job roles carefully.

TIP

BE ENTHUSIASTIC
Give full attention and energy to your own job role. Only then will you be able to understand and design a suitable job role for your employees.

Making a job role motivational

You may work in a pleasant environment, but if you see no purpose in your job, you are unlikely to be motivated. This is why it is so important to design a job role suitable for each employee. In a job that is designed well, the jobholder should be able to use a variety of skills in their job, be involved in the whole activity, and have a meaningful role in which they understand the impact of the work they do. You should give your staff freedom to carry out tasks and provide them with regular feedback on what they are doing well, in addition to where they could improve.

Improving a job role

Few managers have the opportunity to design a job role from scratch. Unless you are embarking on a major change program, any new job will almost certainly have to fit in with the current structure. However, you can make changes that will have a significant effect on motivation in your team. Every individual has different strengths and skills. If you understand what these are, you may be able to allocate the work in your team to play to someone's strengths. Bring your team together and ask them to think about their jobs and how they could be better designed. Be careful, though, because any changes have to be made in the light of the overall effectiveness of the organization. For example, deciding you will unilaterally agree on a policy of flexible working for your team is probably not a good idea for the organization as a whole. An effective way of improving existing jobs is job rotation—moving people around so they develop a broader range of skills and gain experience of doing other jobs. Job enrichment is a means of giving people greater depth rather than breadth in their roles. It is about giving them more responsibility, autonomy, and discretion. This is often done to add interest where people are in very straightforward jobs.

TIP

ASSESS YOUR OWN ROLE
Think about your role. What do you like about it? What do you not like? Can you change it? Does it give you any pointers as to how your staff members perceive their own roles?

ASK YOURSELF... HOW DO I DEFINE A ROLE?

- What is the tangible outcome of the role?
- What would happen if the role did not exist?
- What place does the role have in the structure of the organization?
- Do I know my employees well enough to design a suitable role for them?
- Could the role be broken down and shared among existing employees?
- Can I enrich the existing job role?
- How will the results of the jobholder's contribution be measured?

Creating a balance

In motivating people to perform well, you should aim to balance high performance with constructive behavior as well as balance short-term success with achieving longer-term goals. It is also important to give equal weight to the needs of the organization and the individual.

Balancing performance indicators and behavior

*Gaming—the behavior associated with achieving the target numbers by any means and without regard for delivering real performance.

Most measurements of performance don't give a view of the future. Take the sales target as an example. Close to the month end, a salesman may make unrealistic promises to his customers and take orders that will allow him to reach his bonus. This will ensure achievement of the performance target, but his behavior may upset the customer in the longer term, causing his customer to place their business elsewhere. This behavior is gaming* the system and as a manager you need to take steps to prevent this.

Balancing short- and long-term needs

TIP

CHOOSE YOUR STYLE

In a crisis, short-term motivational techniques will be most appropriate, but make sure you return to long-term techniques when the crisis is over.

Motivation has short- and long-term elements. In the short term, commitment, direction, and enthusiasm will motivate people. But in the longer term, people need to see they are being led and that changes are being made to help them do their work. In the longer term, giving people the right tools, creating the right working environment, and giving them the training they need is much more motivational. Short-term success has to be translated into long-term success by changing the way the work is done.

Blake–Mouton management grid

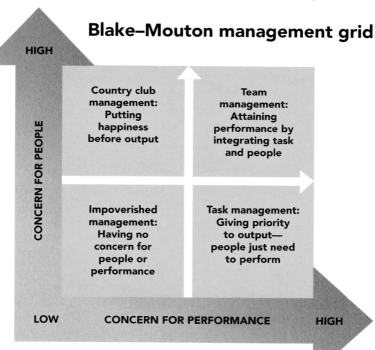

HIGH

CONCERN FOR PEOPLE

Country club management: Putting happiness before output

Team management: Attaining performance by integrating task and people

Impoverished management: Having no concern for people or performance

Task management: Giving priority to output—people just need to perform

LOW   **CONCERN FOR PERFORMANCE**   HIGH

Balancing work and individual needs

Ask yourself whether you are people-focused or task-focused. Do you devote most of your effort to achieving the goals that have been set for the organization, or do you focus on making sure that people are content in their jobs? In reality, you should do both. The organization needs to achieve its goals and targets, so these are important.

However, the people who work for the organization have their own needs and these can't be ignored. The key to motivational management is to align your employees' needs closely with those of the organization. Management theorists Robert Blake and Jane Mouton created a grid that reflects four approaches to management. They suggest managers should aim to be in the top right-hand box, showing high concern for both people and performance.

Conducting appraisals

An appraisal is a formal process for setting objectives, measuring progress, and providing feedback to employees on performance. When conducted in an appropriate manner, it can motivate individuals to perform more effectively and progress within the organization.

Benefiting from appraisals

One of the key benefits of the appraisal process is that it provides a structured approach to managing performance. This is important because personal objectives are essential to guiding motivation. It also forces managers to sit down and have a frank discussion with each team member. It is important not to rely on the appraisals alone to manage your team; you will need to monitor performance regularly and communicate informally as well. However, having an organization-wide mechanism for managing performance and career aspirations is invaluable.

REVIEWING
Assess the individual's performance and discuss their career aspirations.

Focusing on the "how"

Appraisals normally consist of formal meetings between the individual and their immediate manager, focusing on objectives and their progress. Discuss how the objective is being achieved as well as what has been achieved. The "how" is essential for long-term success. If an individual has achieved a high level of output but has poached resources from other teams to achieve this, take this into account while assessing performance.

KEEPING A RECORD
Write out detailed notes of issues discussed and action points for the future.

Elements of an appraisal

SETTING GOALS
Review progress against current objectives and set new objectives that are linked to the organization's goals.

ANALYSIS
Consider development needs for the current role and future progression if appropriate.

EXAMINATION
Talk about more intangible issues, such as how objectives have been achieved.

COMMUNICATION
Discuss specific problems, especially those that have prevented your employee from meeting an objective.

Setting objectives

Setting objectives is one of the most difficult tasks a manager faces. If the objectives are too hard, people can become demotivated, but if they are too easy, people coast along. Objective setting takes time and effort, but it is the only real way of directing your staff.

EVALUATE THE OBJECTIVES

There is a saying "what gets measured gets done," so make sure the goals you set correspond with what you want the individual to deliver.

Setting objectives in context

Everybody in your organization is dependent on the efforts of other people, so, in setting objectives, you need to take account of the context. For example, the sales team is often seen as a department where targets are achieved solely through the efforts of the sales people, but this is not the case. The team that processes the orders is also important, as are those that designed and created a good product. Motivating people to exert higher levels of effort will improve performance, but in many administrative, service, and manufacturing jobs the system has a much greater impact on the level of output than the effort of individual employees. As a manager you will need to keep this in mind while setting goals for your employees to steer clear of unrealistic expectations from your staff.

Linking objectives to strategy

SET RELEVANT GOALS

Make sure you don't set objectives just because they are easily measurable. Always ask yourself if the objective really matters.

People are motivated when their objectives are linked to the overall goals of the organization and they can see how they contribute to the organization's success. Without this line of sight, people can easily lose their sense of purpose at work, which can adversely affect their motivation. Cascade the objectives down through the organization, with each department having a stated aim and a set of goals that must be reached to achieve the overall objective.

Achieving objectives through targets

Break down objectives into individual targets that can be used as measures of performance. For example, the objective might be to improve the quality of customer service in a restaurant, and the targets following from that might be to have all diners seated within five minutes of their arrival, to have orders transmitted to the kitchen within five minutes of being taken, and to clear tables within five minutes of the diners vacating them.

Creating stretch goals

Stretch goals are goals that are demanding, but not impossible to reach—often described as "high but achievable." You will need to be careful when you set these goals to make them work. Here are some tips to help you avoid the pitfalls:
• Understanding past performance will be important— you should know what your employee is capable of if you want to set a stretch goal. Your employee may well be aiming to set an easier target, so there is a limit to how much you can rely on their input.
• Targets are usually set in advance for the year, but circumstances can change rapidly in a volatile environment. To keep your people focused and motivated, be prepared to be flexible and reset the targets to maintain the stretch.
• Targets need to be seen as being fair. The degree of difficulty should be the same for all. Often, the targets you set across your team will vary from individual to individual, according to the requirements of the task and the team's overall capabilities. Explain carefully why the targets have been set. If they are perceived as being unequal, they will cause friction and demotivation.

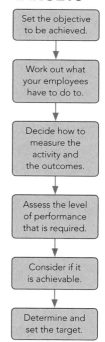

HOW TO... SET TARGETS

Set the objective to be achieved.

↓

Work out what your employees have to do to.

↓

Decide how to measure the activity and the outcomes.

↓

Assess the level of performance that is required.

↓

Consider if it is achievable.

↓

Determine and set the target.

TIP

EQUIP YOUR STAFF
Consider what people need to do their job. It is frustrating if you can't perform because of lack of equipment.

Creating personal objectives

Not all the objectives you set should be linked to short-term performance outcomes. There must be a balance between the needs of the organization and those of the individual. Training and development may take your staff away from their day-to-day job and may require the organization to spend money. However, setting a personal development goal is motivational because it demonstrates the organization is interested in the individual and their long-term career. As part of the appraisal process, discuss the employees' skills and development needs in the longer term, and include these in their personal objectives.

TIP

PULL TOGETHER
Allocate a shared objective to several people. The benefits of working as a team outweigh the motivation of individual objectives.

Communicating the objectives

How you set objectives is very important. Set targets face to face with your employees. This will allow you to explain what the targets are and discuss their feasibility and implications. To be motivational, objectives need to be owned, so discuss them with your employees to get feedback. This will help you gauge whether they are prepared to accept the objective. Choose a suitable channel to communicate with them. If you distribute the sales targets for the year by email, it will tell everyone what is required, but does little for motivation. If you manage too many people to see them all individually, consider how to reorganize the reporting relationship to make sure each individual is managed properly.

Defining a S.U.S.T.A.I.N.A.B.L.E objective

STRETCHING
It requires commitment and effort

UNDERSTOOD
Employees know what has to be achieved,
what is required, and why it is important

SUPPORTED
It includes a plan of action that should ensure success

TIME BOUND
Everyone knows what has to be achieved by when

ACHIEVABLE
It is realistic within resource and time constraints

INCLUSIVE
It draws colleagues into achieving the goal

NEGOTIATED
Objectives are agreed on rather than imposed

ANSWERABLE
Performance outcome, not the activity, is measured

BELIEVED
It is seen as the right objective
to be achieved

LINKED
It is consistent with the
organization's goals

EXPLAINED
It is clearly stated
with measurable
outcomes

Measuring progress

Feedback is an important element of motivation. Once objectives have been set it is important that you track and monitor progress and discuss it with your staff. But you also need to know when to intervene and when to leave a situation alone.

Measuring key activities

*KPI— "Key Performance Indicator." KPIs track performance of the organization against its higher-level goals.

The usual way of measuring progress is to plot a graph of KPIs*, such as monthly sales figures, against the target. But not all progress can be tracked so simply—some projects require considerable input before change in the output can be measured. To avoid demotivating your staff, you need to measure progress against each of the activities that contributes to achieving the outcome.

Feeding back results

Measurement provides feedback and feedback should be acted on. For the measurement to be motivational, make sure those being measured see the results and understand how they were calculated. If this doesn't happen, they will not know how to improve their performance. Ideally, people need to measure their own performance, so feedback is instantaneous. This way the individual or team can see quickly how they are progressing, allowing them to act even before management is alerted to a problem. For example, keeping a graph of calls handled or components produced provides feedback in real time. But you can't measure progress on all aspects of your work. Sometimes others have to measure your work for you—many accounting measures fall into this category.

TIP

REGULATE

Measure often, but be aware that if you measure too often, you may not be able to detect any change.

Choosing the right measure

You need to choose the correct indicator to measure your employees' performance. For instance, how would you assess the performance of a maintenance team? Is it good if they are constantly busy and working long hours? Does this show how motivated they are? If they are all sitting around is it because they are lazy and demotivated? In fact, you want your maintenance team to be idle most of the time because this means all the equipment is working and your factory is producing. Be careful to choose the correct measure, and not to confuse high levels of activity with performance.

ASK YOURSELF... AM I MEASURING CORRECTLY?

- Do I have a clear measure of performance?
- Do I have a clear measure of activity?
- Do I know how much effort is required to perform well?
- Do I review performance regularly?
- Do I give feedback regularly?
- Do I use the measures of performance in formal reviews?
- Do I use the measures to make decisions?
- Do I communicate performance indicators to all those involved?
- Do I make sure all those involved understand what the performance is and how we deliver it?
- Do I understand the external factors that affect the performance being measured?

CASE STUDY

"Andon" way of measuring

Many Japanese car manufacturers use an "Andon" system on their production lines. This system allows a worker to stop the whole production line because he has encountered a problem he can't solve himself. When this process was adopted in a European car plant, the flashing lights triggered by the Andon system brought all the managers down onto the factory floor. They would remain there to provide support and motivation until the plant restarted. As problems reduced and the Andon system was used less often, managers stayed away. This was a sign of success, but the production workers didn't see it that way. They lost touch with their managers, which made them feel neglected and less inclined to use the system when things went wrong. The company eventually realized their mistake and made sure management discussed and reviewed progress with the production workers regularly and, most importantly, celebrated success together.

Training and development

Research has shown that employees, particularly young people, value development opportunities. A company that offers training and development is showing commitment to its employees, developing them for the future, and helping them do a better job in the process.

TIP

MATCH TRAINING WITH ABILITY

Some people prefer to learn by "doing" and others are happy to read about a subject or listen to a lecture, so consider what you want the training to achieve, and then establish how the individual learns best.

Making the case for training

Training should be encouraged so that it is woven into the culture of the organization. Having a good training program and being aware of development needs are excellent ways of attracting the best people to join your organization, motivating them, and also retaining them. This can give a business a substantial advantage over its competitors. It is essential that the training itself is of a high standard, otherwise it is a waste of time. Though the appraisal meeting provides a formal opportunity for the individual and manager to discuss training, development needs arise throughout the year and should be addressed from time to time to ensure success. You must also make sure the training meets the employee's own development needs to keep them motivated.

Getting the best from training

Any type of training involves spending time or money (and usually both), so it is important to be sure you derive maximum benefit from it. Make sure you seek out underlying needs, suited to the individual's job role. For example, if they are learning a skill, make sure they will be able to practice it. Having established these, you should brief the individual beforehand on what they can expect from the training. Discuss afterward what they have learned and how they should use it.

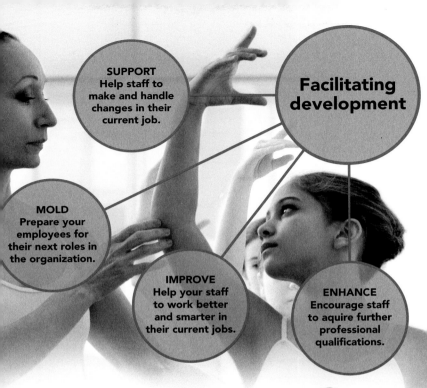

SUPPORT
Help staff to make and handle changes in their current job.

Facilitating development

MOLD
Prepare your employees for their next roles in the organization.

IMPROVE
Help your staff to work better and smarter in their current jobs.

ENHANCE
Encourage staff to aquire further professional qualifications.

Exploring ways of development

Rather than sending employees for external training, you can consider other methods of development:
• **Job rotation** Moving around the organization to learn different jobs and acquire new skills and knowledge in the process.
• **Lateral transfer** Working in another department on a project, to give a broader perspective to their work.
• **Coaching and mentoring** Receiving one-to-one support from a more experienced colleague.
• **Professional certification** A degree or certificate in marketing or finance can provide a life-time benefit. This requires a lot of of time and effort, so both the individual and the organization must be ready to commit.

TIP

MANAGE EXPECTATIONS

Increase your employees' prospects in the organization after they complete the training by offering them more responsibility, or they might look for a better opportunity somewhere else.

Recognizing performance

Most people think money is the key motivator and reward for good performance. It isn't. It may be motivating to have a pay raise or bonus but the effects are often short-lived. Simple recognition is a very powerful motivator, and can and should occur every day. Just praising someone who is doing something well can make all the difference, and costs nothing.

TIP

USE INGENIOUS WAYS TO PRAISE
Make praise public. For example, print out customer commendations and place them on the bulletin board for everyone to see.

Giving recognition

Everyone likes to receive a thank you and to get credit for work well done. Identifying when things have been done well and recognizing this formally is an excellent way of motivating on a day-to-day basis.

All organizations should make sure that the basics of recognition, such as saying "thank you," are ingrained in all employees. However, many companies also run formal recognition systems. These tend to reward the teams or individuals with the greatest output, those who have built good relationships with their customers, and those who have supported their colleagues most.

Recognition, whether formal or informal, is a way of ensuring that people, and managers in particular, are always keeping an eye out for good performance, and promote it around the company. Here are some other ways to recognize the efforts of your employees:

- Send them an email thanking them for their support.
- Copy their boss into the thank-you email.
- Take them (or the team) out for a drink after work.
- Buy them and their partner dinner.
- Give them a bouquet of flowers or a box of chocolates with a note.
- Explain at the team meeting what they did and why it was so good.
- Create a program for "employee of the month."
- Give them half a day off.
- Make sure that your team celebrates success.

Using the personal touch

Informal recognition systems may rely on local management initiative, but they are essential. They require managers to know what is going on and to be able to spot good work and high levels of effort. As a manager, you need to be involved in what your employees are doing and saying. This, in itself, is motivating to your staff, who see that you are interested in their work.

However, be aware that recognition is not as simple as saying "thank you"—people can see when you aren't being sincere. It is important to react spontaneously when you notice their efforts and mean what you say. Tell your boss about employees who perform well—being perceived positively by the senior management will boost their morale. Your staff will also appreciate it if you make a personal effort to recognize good performance by thanking them face-to-face. If appropriate, consider an inexpensive gift such as flowers or chocolates, although if you start doing this, make it a policy for all high-performing employees, to avoid accusations of favoritism.

✔ CHECKLIST RECOGNIZING WORK

	YES	NO
• Do you always say thank you?	☐	☐
• Do you always make a positive comment when work is done well?	☐	☐
• Do you try to catch your staff doing something well every week?	☐	☐
• When you see exceptional performance, do you tell everyone?	☐	☐
• Do you buy a small gift to say thank you when appropriate?	☐	☐
• Do you exploit the formal recognition system for good performance?	☐	☐

Paying for performance

Pay is often used as a motivator. It can take the form of salary increases, commission, or bonuses. Rules can be set in advance for deciding how much is paid using a particular formula, or a judgment can be made at the end of the year as to how much is deserved.

TIP

STAY ON TRACK

Always link bonuses back to what the organization is trying to achieve in the long run. If you don't, you will be rewarding behavior that is not benefiting the organization.

Motivating through pay

The motivational element of pay comes from linking the level of financial return to the performance of an individual or team. The intention is to motivate people to put in more effort because they know they will receive a greater financial reward. Here are some other reasons for linking pay and performance:
• To conform to the standard in the industry
• To manage costs—pay is given in proportion to the financial results received.

Linking pay and performance

To link pay and performance, you must be able to measure the element of performance you wish to reward objectively. You need to select the elements you reward with care—if you reward only one element of performance you will need other management approaches to ensure other aspects are not neglected. Fairness is one of the most important factors in linking performance with reward. When the system is seen to be fair, people will be motivated. If people work independently, then reward the individual for his or her performance. If team effort is required, you must reward the team effort. Target setting is the most difficult aspect of linking pay to performance. You will need to collect enough data to be sure your target is both stretching and attainable.

METHODS OF LINKING PAY AND PERFORMANCE

METHOD	POSITIVE IMPACT	NEGATIVE IMPACT
Directly linking bonus to achieving specific targets	• Makes the reward mechanism very clear • Encourages very specific behavior	• Can become very rigid and therefore irrelevant if circumstances at the workplace change
Indirectly linking bonus and pay to performance	• Allows managers to exercise their judgment • Allows a more rounded view of performance	• Makes the reward mechanism less clear
Setting targets through consultation	• Motivates people through engagement in the target-setting process	• Can become a negotiation • Will encourage people to set easy targets • Will encourage people to hoard (rather than share) information
Linking size of incentive to goals	• Large incentives will be acted on • Small incentives help communication of goals	• Large incentives may encourage cheating • Small incentives may fail to motivate people
Paying a bonus when a fixed-value target is achieved	• The threshold target becomes specific and is easy to comprehend	• There is no incentive to perform once the target is reached • There is no incentive to perform if the target becomes unattainable • Encourages gaming—the pulling forward and putting back of performance between periods to achieve the bonus
Paying a bonus at each step toward achieving a target	• Creates an incentive to perform over a range of outcomes • Rewards high performers for their work	• Sets a less specific expectation
Linking performance to salary increases	• Reduces costs as increments are usually smaller than bonus payments	• Invariably, such increases are paid for the rest of the employee's time of service
Setting targets afterward by comparison with others	• Makes targets appropriate in nearly all circumstances	• Makes the link between effort and performance, and performance and reward, less clear

Chapter 3

Developing the skills of motivation

Once you have learned the principles of motivation and how to create the right environment for it to flourish, you need to develop the skills to motivate your team. It is important to practice these skills continually to increase your capability.

Motivating yourself

As a manager, you are a role model. Your staff will notice what you say, how you say it, and how you behave. It is important that you are motivated yourself. Remember that the principles of motivation apply just as much to you as they do to your team.

Understanding what you want

TIP

BE PROACTIVE

If you don't like something and you can change it or think it can be changed, take positive action.

It is worth thinking about what you really want. This will help motivate you and enable you to structure your ambitions and goals. Understanding what you want applies to your personal life as much as your work life—the two are intertwined. If you really want to spend more time with your family then you are unlikely to be motivated if you are in a job where you are required to spend many hours at work. If you come to the conclusion that you're not in the right job, you are better off moving to a new job that suits your circumstances better.

Knowing what motivates you

Most people are so busy with their day-to-day activities they don't take the time to reflect on what they enjoy doing. Everyone has to do tasks they don't like, but if you can build several tasks you really enjoy into your day, it will help keep you motivated. Think about your work—what aspects do you enjoy? Is it contact with people? Writing a report? Creating a new idea? Can you do more of these activities? What do you not enjoy? Can you minimize the time you spend on these tasks in future? Is there a better way of doing them? It is easy to put off tasks you don't enjoy doing, but this is a mistake because the thought of doing them remains on your mind. The trick is to do them, get them out of the way, and start something you really want to do that will motivate you.

Setting your own goals

Set goals for yourself, just as you would for your staff. This gives you something to aim for. Make sure your goals mean something to you, to give you a sense of achievement. Be precise and set a timeframe, so you can monitor your progress. If the goal is large, break it down into manageable chunks. Don't say "I will increase my personal network of contacts"; say instead, "I will add five new contacts to my personal network from the construction sector by the end of December."

Goals don't have to be totally work-related. In fact, it is a good idea to have some personal goals. For example, you might decide you need to lose weight or get into better shape. In this case, one of your goals might be to lose 10lb (4.5kg) or to participate in some organized runs by a certain date.

To give yourself some extra motivation to achieve your chosen goals, spend some time visualizing what it will be like when you have achieved them.

Dealing with problems

From time to time, problems will arise at work. They generally fall into two groups: those you can ease or solve and those you can do nothing about. It is no use worrying about something you cannot change. Recognize this, work around it, and carry on as best as you can without brooding. If the problem is beyond your control but very important to you, speak to your boss. If possible, come up with a solution yourself and suggest it to them.

Learning from mistakes

It is easy to lose motivation when you have made a mistake, but remember that no one is perfect. If you aren't making any mistakes, it probably means you aren't taking any risks and are staying within your "comfort zone." If a mistake occurs, do not make excuses or blame someone else. Accept constructive criticism, learn what you can from it, and move on.

DEALING WITH CRITICISM

FAST TRACK	OFF TRACK
Listening to what is being said	Becoming defensive
Making sure you understand what you are being criticized for	Focusing on failure
Seeking clarification if necessary	Taking it personally
Reflecting on the action to take	Dwelling on past problems

Being positive

If all you do is complain about problems and always appear negative, you will have no hope of motivating your staff. But this does not mean you always have to be cheerful and only see the advantages in everything around you. It is important to be realistic. If you have started a project and you can see problems with it, your first task is to find ways of resolving them. If the problems really can't be resolved, you will probably have to work around them. Let your staff know what the problems are, but also reassure them you will help work through them. Make sure they know what your expectations are of them.

TIP

STAY POSITIVE
Concentrate on the good things you have done. Build up a store of positive experiences and keep these in your mind.

Balancing work and life

Successful people usually have a wide range of hobbies and interests outside work, together with a broad network of friends and contacts. It is often helpful to share problems with people away from your place of work because they see them in a new light. Even if you thoroughly enjoy your job, do not become a workaholic. If you spend all your time concentrating on your work you will eventually become tired, dissatisfied, and demotivated.

Being a good motivator

Motivation is not just about understanding and applying the theories—it is about how you put them into practice. In essence, being a good motivator is part of being a good leader—someone people will follow. For this to happen, you need the personal characteristics that make people want to follow you.

TIP

BE AWARE
Pay attention to what is going on around you to understand what motivates your staff, but make sure you don't get involved in gossip.

Knowing what makes a good motivator

There is no single "good" management style that will turn you into a good motivator. If you try to adopt a style with which you feel uncomfortable, you will come across as being insincere and you won't be trusted. However, there are some characteristics all good motivators share. It is worth reflecting on the people you believe are good motivators. What was it about them that spurred you on to achieve? This will give you an insight into your own personal motivation, as well as helping you consider how you can motivate your team.

✔ CHECKLIST ARE YOU A GOOD MOTIVATOR?

	YES	NO
• Can you be trusted—do what you say you will do?	☐	☐
• Can you build rapport with individuals on the team?	☐	☐
• Are you loyal to your team?	☐	☐
• Are you fair in your dealings with people?	☐	☐
• Do you share credit with the team for achievements?	☐	☐
• Can you see the individual's perspective while keeping the organization's goal in mind?	☐	☐

Balancing trust and authority

One of the most important characteristics of good motivators is that they can be trusted. It is only possible to motivate people for a very short time without gaining their trust. To gain the trust of your team, never make promises you can't keep because, if you let people down, they will be very wary in the future. If something goes wrong, it is your job as the leader of the team to take responsibility and criticism for it. You have to defend your team in public while investigating in private what went wrong and how it can be avoided in future. As a manager, you have a difficult balance to strike between "being one of the team" and being the leader. Quite where this balance will lie will depend on the structure and culture of the organization. Some have very "flat" structures where there is very little difference between managers and their staff—others have more hierarchy. Whatever the culture in your organization, some distance should be maintained, or your own authority can be undermined, making it difficult for you to manage problems with poor performers. If there is too much distance, however, you will never get to know individuals on your team, and they won't know whether they can trust you or not.

Focusing on the future

As a manager, you need to organize and take care of detail, but someone who spends all their time on this without seeing the wider context is unlikely to be a good motivator. You need to know how reaching your immediate goal will lead to achieving the ultimate objective. An often-quoted example of this is two bricklayers who are asked what they are doing. "I'm laying bricks," says one. The other says "I'm building a cathedral." A good motivator will paint a picture of the objective to strengthen their team's sense of purpose.

TIP

EMPATHIZE WITH YOUR STAFF
Understanding your team's problems and empathizing with their position will help you motivate them better.

HOW TO... MOTIVATE YOUR STAFF

Share the vision with your team.

↓

Make the goals real to your people.

↓

Give regular feedback to your staff.

↓

Recognize performance.

↓

Celebrate success with all those involved.

Making people feel valued

If people feel valued by their manager, they will be prepared to make the extra effort that can make the difference between success and failure. However, in facing the day-to-day pressures of meeting deadlines and trying to achieve targets, many managers overlook the relatively small actions that show they value the individuals in their team.

Understanding the benefits

New employees are usually brimming with enthusiasm when they join an organization or begin a new role. But somewhere along the line, it is common for most staff to suffer from demotivation. If the organization fails to value its staff, why should they contribute whole-heartedly to the organization's success? Although "valuing someone" may sound intangible and fluffy, research shows employees who are valued perform better in their job and this, in turn, leads to higher levels of business performance.

REWARD
Not every organization can pay the best wages in the industry but it is important that your staff members are rewarded fairly for their work, they understand the organization's policy and see it is applied consistently.

IN FOCUS... COMMITMENT-BASED HR

Researchers have defined two types of HR practice: commitment based and transaction based. Commitment-based practices focus on developing the long-term relationship between the employer and the employee in an organization. Mentoring, training, and development are all examples of commitment-based practices.

Transaction-based practices focus on the here and now, just paying people for the work they do. A recent study in the UK showed that commitment-based practices increased employee engagement, which led to higher levels of product and service quality, innovation, and better financial performance.

RECOGNITION
Simply saying thank you when people are doing things well and taking the trouble to show you appreciate them form the first step in valuing people.

PERSONAL TOUCH
Getting to know people as individuals so they feel you are taking an interest in them personally is vitally important. But make sure you extend the same level of interest and flexibility to all members of your team. It is easy to slip into the habit of favoritism.

Techniques for making staff feel valued

POWER OF EXPRESSION
Employees feel valued if their opinions are heard and taken into account during decision-making.

TRAINING AND DEVELOPMENT
People feel valued if the organization invests in them and in their future. Organizations that invest in people find that people commit to them, so training and development become essential.

PROMOTION
People who perform well will look to progress in their career. Helping them in that progression demonstrates your commitment to them.

Developing communication

Communication and openness are important tools for motivation. If you don't communicate effectively, people will feel unimportant and undervalued. Ambiguous communication can also lead to the spread of rumors, which is unhealthy because rumors play on people's fears.

Sharing information

There is a balance between sharing what you know and worrying people unnecessarily. In some cases it is important first to consider the consequences of sharing information. Unless you are at the stage of consulting people, it is sometimes better to wait until you have some tangible ideas to put forward. Putting forward fuzzy thoughts rarely leads to people feeling they are being kept informed. They are more likely to think you are hiding something. However, it is better to err on the side of overcommunicating than to hold information back.

Communicating well

Communication is a two-way process. It is not just about telling people something—it is also about listening to what is being said. Good motivators are people who think about what they are saying and how they are saying it. They constantly gauge the response from their listeners, and when they have spoken, they keep quiet and listen. In this way they gain insights into how people are feeling and receive new ideas and perspectives. Practice listening and you will be surprised by how much you can learn.

BE A GOOD LISTENER
Look at the speaker, lean forward, and encourage them by nodding your head. Good listeners will also ask questions and seek clarification if they do not understand a point.

Selecting the right channel

How you communicate is just as important as what you communicate, so it is essential to think carefully about which communication channel to use. Everyone is different—some people prefer to read information, others to hear it. If you have something important to say it is a good idea to use several different communication channels to strengthen your message and appeal to people in different ways. Having a one-to-one meeting is good for dealing with individual problems but can be time consuming, while a team meeting allows discussion of issues and facilitates mutual understanding. The telephone is a convenient way to give information that is easy to understand. Emails, newsletters, and the intranet are impersonal but provide an instant means of reaching a large number of people.

Managing politics

Politics in the workplace are difficult to avoid. Whatever you do, cliques will form, people will jockey for position, and rumors will be spread. In the longer term this leads to energy being diverted away from the business and can even lead to victimization and bullying of individuals. It is important you know what is going on and put a stop to it. Politics can undermine the positive culture of the organization, and damage motivation. Bullying has the same effect, so when you detect this happening, act quickly and prevent it from happening in the future. Plug yourself into your organization's networks so you understand what is going on, but avoid letting it distract you from your own work.

Identifying demotivation

Demotivation in the workplace has a wide variety of causes, from tiredness and overwork to problems at home. Demotivated employees can affect the morale of their colleagues, and whole teams can also become demotivated, so it is essential to be able to recognize the signs of demotivation and to act quickly.

Pinpointing the signs

Everyone has days when they feel demotivated and below par. Demotivation may not always be immediately apparent but there are some signs to watch out for. An employee may be slumped at their desk, gazing into space, or tapping their fingers on the desk. You can also tell how they are feeling from the tone of their voice. A monotonous tone or yawning may be signals that someone is bored or tired. While these are not always signs of serious demotivation and you shouldn't be too quick to jump to conclusions, you should still check them out. Other signs of demotivation include people who normally react well to requests failing to respond or avoiding volunteering for new tasks. Don't let too much time pass before you act. Anyone can have an off day, but if it persists, or there is a regular pattern to their mood swings, then you should talk to the individual concerned. If they feel overworked, see if you can reallocate some of their tasks. Saying you appreciate what they have been doing can be enough to raise their spirits and remotivate them. Even a quick "How are things today?" shows you have noticed and care about how they are feeling.

Dealing with performance issues

One of the most noticeable signs of more serious problems is when someone who is normally a good worker fails to perform. Of course, this may just be a one-time occurance. Perhaps the individual has had a particularly difficult task to do or a difficult customer to deal with. But if their work is constantly below their normal standard, there is a problem you need to tackle. Neither will this type of problem be solved by a quick question about how the person is, nor will it be solved by a military-style inquisition. You will need an in-depth discussion to identify what is wrong and what can be done to put it right. Discuss the problem in a confidential meeting, set targets for improving performance, and agree on a strategy to resolve it.

TIP

ACT QUICKLY

If you detect the signs of demotivation in one of your employees, their colleagues will see them, too. Don't ignore the signs. Take action quickly before the team thinks you haven't noticed or don't care.

Countering absenteeism

High levels of staff absenteeism are a strong sign of a demotivated team. To deal with this, talk to staff after every absence. Meet with every absent staff member, so you cannot be accused of singling anyone out, but make the discussion private, so you can adapt your approach depending on how often the individual is absent and the underlying cause. The objective of the meeting is twofold: first, so your staff members are aware that you have noted absences, and second, to ascertain the cause. Finding out why people are absent is the first step to tackling the problem.

Be aware of staff turnover. Even if the figure for your department is below average, make sure you know why people are leaving. New staff bring in new ideas, but high levels of staff turnover unsettle a team and can demotivate those left behind. Your organization's human resources team should always conduct exit interviews to establish why someone is leaving, and you must be sure the feedback is passed on to you.

Consulting others

Consultation plays an important part in motivation. Jointly setting goals and targets with others communicates what is to be achieved and increases their commitment to achieving them. So consult when you can, but realize that if you have to make a quick decision it is not always possible.

OPEN IT UP
Involve people in making decisions whenever you can. Teams often make better decisions than individuals.

Involving people

Think about how you feel when you are told about decisions that directly affect you at work. How would you feel if they were announced with no prior warning or consultation? Sometimes it can be a pleasant surprise, but often you feel bewildered: "Why did they do that? What a stupid decision!" Now think about the decision on which you have been consulted or involved. You know why the decision was made, and although you may not have fully agreed with it, you won't think it is stupid. Consulting avoids the instant negative impact on morale and performance.

BE CLEAR
People need to know when you are giving orders and when you are consulting. Make this absolutely clear or you will cause confusion.

Benefiting from consultation

You will benefit from consulting with others because:
• You can involve others in the process of setting goals and agreeing on actions, drawing them into the process and increasing their commitment to the project.
• You will gain information from other persepectives, on the basis of which you can decide and act.
• You and your team will improve your understanding of what has to be achieved, and why.
• It can help you in setting targets at the right level.
• The whole process can be motivational and help strengthen bonds within your teams.
• The final agreement strengthens the commitment of the team, ensuring they will perform.

KNOWING WHEN TO CONSULT

CONSULT...	DON'T CONSULT...
• When you have the time to consult.	• When people are expecting to be told what to do.
• When there is still time to influence the decision.	• When quick decisive action is needed.
• When your team's input will improve the decision.	• When the decision has already been made.
• When you need the team to agree on the project's goal for its success.	• When there is an obvious technical expert whose advice you should follow.

Avoiding pitfalls

There are a number of pitfalls when consulting. It is important that people know when they are being consulted and when they are being informed of a decision. Some targets are not negotiable—they have been set high up in the company and allocated to your team. If you are going to consult in this situation you will need to explain that the target is not up for negotiation, but you want input on how it is going to be met. Ask yourself whether the consultation is genuine and not a public-relations exercise. If there is little likelihood of the organization taking into account what is being discussed, you must still take feedback from your staff so they can let off steam, but also explain to them that while you will pass their comments on, you don't expect things to change as a result.

CASE STUDY

You don't know what you don't know

An electricity distribution company faced the issue of needing to undertake maintenance on its power lines but having to compensate customers every time the power was cut off. Staff worked quickly on the repairs, but the costs were high. In order to cascade the strategy down the organization, the objective of reducing the cost was delegated to the front-line maintenance team. They came up with the solution of buying a generator so the electric supply could be maintained while the repairs were made. When this was proposed to the finance director, his immediate reply was "Do you know what a generator costs?" They didn't, but he didn't know the cost of cutting the supply. The new generator cost $1 million, but by consulting the front-line staff and involving them in the decision-making process, the company rapidly paid off the cost of the generator and made significant savings.

Delegating effectively

Delegating tasks is not only a way to reduce your workload, but it can also motivate employees. However, while having a task delegated to you can be a highly motivating experience, it can also result in loss of confidence and demotivation if you are unable to complete the task.

Knowing when to delegate

While delegation reduces your workload, it also means letting go of the task and giving it to someone else. This means you should only delegate tasks with a clear structure. Implement a monitoring process so you can assure yourself progress is being made and the person is comfortable with the task at hand. Delegate when the task is likely to be repeated, making it worth the time and effort, or when the task itself may be motivating for someone else to do. Avoid delegating if there are time constraints or the individual does not have the necessary skill or experience.

5
SUPPORT
Encourage and guide the individual or team, give feedback regularly, and keep checking on progress.

Deciding how to delegate

How to delegate will depend on the working environment, how well you know the person you are delegating to, their level of experience, and the importance of the task. Delegation takes time to do well. With an experienced team, it can be done over a cup of coffee, but if you have a critical project or you are working with people you don't know well, it is better to be formal. Ideally, this should involve a face-to-face meeting supported by an email or document recording what has been agreed upon. Be sure you have allocated the time both to hand over the task and to follow it up.

Delegating efficiently

1 IDENTIFY
Define the task, check that all the required resources are available, and specify the desired outcomes.

2 DISTRIBUTE
Decide who you are going to assign the task to and allocate the resources in a judicious manner.

3 BRIEF
Communicate and agree on the goals with your employees. Try to delegate a whole task rather than part of it.

4 MONITOR
Make sure each employee who has been delegated a specific part of the task is performing.

Coaching successfully

There are many different forms of coaching but, in essence, coaching at work is about having a series of conversations with someone to help them perform better in their job. It is also a highly effective way of motivating them by focusing on their needs.

Coaching on a daily basis

Many people think of coaching as a special form of training undertaken only by a specialized coach. In many cases it is. As a manager, however, you will need to understand the principles of coaching and build them into your day-to-day work. You may want to coach someone for a specific task or prepare them to take on a more senior role. Coach the individuals in your team so they can handle their own work independently. In addition to motivating them, this saves you time by enabling them to take responsibility for their own work.

Being a good coach

Assist your employees throughout the duration of the task and keep giving them feedback.

Make observations on someone's behavior, which they may not have noticed themselves.

Enable your staff to find their own way through a problem and suggest practical solutions.

Encourage individuals or teams to take responsibility for a particular task.

Developing your coaching skills

The fundamental skills of coaching are building trust, listening, and questioning. Put the person at their ease to encourage them to talk. While you need to keep the conversation on track, allow them to speak without interruption as far as possible. Ask questions to help maintain their focus and show you are listening. This will also encourage them to think about better ways of doing things and see issues from a wider perspective. Support them as they try implementing their solutions, and give appropriate feedback.

TIP

STIMULATE VIEWPOINTS

By asking a challenging question, you may help your employees see the issue from a new perspective.

Giving constructive feedback

Feedback is an important part of the coaching process. But make sure it is well intentioned and constructive. You should also try to make it objective and, above all, never personally hurtful. Try to back up what you are saying with some evidence. If the individual has no control over something then there is little point in giving them feedback on it.

GIVING APPROPRIATE FEEDBACK

FAST TRACK	OFF TRACK
Being precise about the feedback	Rushing through what you have to say
Giving the individual time to respond	Giving negative feedback in public
Being constructive	Being uninterested in the way the individual is responding

Chapter 4

Motivating in difficult situations

The environment, processes, and skills of motivation are all important, but some situations will require you to modify your approach. You will need to maintain motivation during change, and in dispersed teams and difficult people.

Motivating during change

Change creates uncertainty for people; it can make them anxious so that they take their eye off the job in question. However, change is increasingly a requirement for organizations to survive. Being able to motivate during change is therefore an extremely important skill.

Recognizing change

Change is rarely popular, and even seemingly trivial innovations in the organization can cause outrage among your staff. Often this is because people don't understand what is happening. This can be avoided if you think through the change in advance and ask yourself two questions:
• Who will this change affect?
• How will the change look from their point of view?
You will then be able to consult those concerned and make sure they are aware of the benefits the change will bring. This process will ensure they stay motivated.

Identifying the types of change

Change can be categorized as either "hard" or "soft." Hard changes are usually well defined in advance. People can be told what will happen and what is expected of them. In a soft change, the details of the change are unknown, and only the direction of the change is clear. The organization has to search for a solution and everyone will have to work through the change together. Major corporate turnarounds often fit this category, as do large-scale cultural change programs*. The best way to cope with a soft change is to become involved, so you have a chance to shape both the change itself and the future of your team.

*Cultural Change Program— program by which the organization tries to change its values and the behavior of its employees.

Being prepared for the change

Be prepared for any kind of response to change and realize that those affected will respond emotionally, and may at times appear irrational. As a manager you can help them to adjust by:
• Accepting the reaction and responding constructively
• Providing information and support
• Creating new roles and objectives
• Giving people a clear vision of the long-term outcomes.

ASK YOURSELF... ARE YOU PREPARED TO MOTIVATE YOUR STAFF THROUGH CHANGE?

• Do I need to introduce different motivational goals for the team?
• Do I need to reset or reemphasize motivational goals for individuals?
• Will my team lose incentives such as bonuses?
• How can I maintain motivation in spite of this?
• Will the current recognition-and-reward system be appropriate after the change?
• If not, what changes in the organization will be required to motivate my team in the new way of working?

TIP

SHOW ENDURANCE

Plan for the downturn in performance associated with change, and absorb some of the frustration and anger.

Recognizing the stages of change

More than half a century ago, the sociologist Kurt Lewin identified three major stages of change. These stages will help you understand the timing of changes, and can be used as a guide for steering people through the process of change.

• **Unfreezing** In this stage you will prepare for change. People will need to recognize the need for the change, and the way things are done will have to be unfrozen, to allow the change to occur. People will be very uncertain during this process.

• **Moving** You will implement the change in this stage by altering working practices, restructuring jobs, or moving people around. People will find everything very new and will need your support and guidance during this process.

• **Refreezing** In this last stage, new ways of working become embedded. During this phase, people should be finding their feet and starting to move forward. The goal of refreezing is to prevent the organization from reverting to its old ways.

The change roller coaster

PERFORMANCE AND SELF-ESTEEM

Uncertainty

Denial

Blaming others

Blaming self

Despair

TIME

Managing the change roller coaster

Different people react to change differently, but during major changes, they go through a series of responses that can be characterized as a "roller coaster ride." This starts with denial, moves on to blaming others, then themselves, which can lead to despair. Self-esteem and performance plummet. However, people then start to test the new environment and ways of working, build confidence, and move on to achieve success. Quite often, once the change has taken place, it is a matter of settling down to the new way of working. You will have to reestablish the culture, rebuild team morale, and reassure individuals. When the change means employees are laid off, make the process as painless as possible. Do everything you can to protect their dignity, and help them take the next steps in their lives.

Performing well

Growing confidence

Testing new ways of working

TIME

Motivating dispersed workers

Developments in technology now enable many people to work from home or in a dispersed team*. In addition, flatter organizational structures mean even larger organizations have local offices employing just a few people. These arrangements bring benefits, such as flexible working hours, but there are serious implications for motivation.

Working away from the office

*Dispersed team—
a team based in a small office out of immediate contact with the main body of the organization.

For many employees, not working in an office is a dream. For the employer it can mean lower office costs and also better productivity because staff don't have to spend time commuting to work.

However, the reality can be less appealing. If you work from home, you can feel isolated, making it hard to stay motivated. Individuals miss the buzz of the office, the companionship of colleagues, and the sparking of ideas when they meet other people. In an office, for example, when something goes wrong, you can turn to a colleague who will help you put the problem in perspective.

Recruiting the right candidate

If a job role will be dispersed or home-based, you should look for certain characteristics at the recruitment stage. If someone lacks self-discipline, cannot manage their time well, or appears to need close supervision, they are unlikely to be suitable. You will need to instill loyalty to be sure they are motivated and focused on the goals to be achieved. At the interview, make sure the candidate is prepared for the working environment. At home this means having room for equipment and a quiet environment. For a dispersed team member, it is the lack of direct supervision and support.

Keeping home workers motivated

A crucial aspect of motivating home workers is to take proactive steps to ensure they have everything they need to work effectively. Agree on targets and time scales and monitor them regularly to check that they are on track. Organize regular visits to the main office, such as monthly team meetings, and arrange one-to-one meetings to catch up on progress and identify any problems before they become too serious. Make sure home- and locally based workers are kept informed of any new developments, and remain in regular contact—not just by email.

EXERCISE TRUST

Trust your home workers or dispersed teams. While you need to know the work is being done, you won't motivate people by checking up on them all the time.

Providing support

To keep your dispersed workers motivated, make sure they feel connected to and supported by the organization as a whole. Arrange a thorough orientation at your main office and make sure your home workers meet the people they will be emailing and speaking to on the phone. You may also need to arrange briefing sessions on working from home. It is particularly important to ensure dispersed teams have all the equipment they need to work effectively. It may be tempting to provide more senior people in head office with the most reliable and expensive IT equipment, but for remote team members, any breakdown is likely to be highly frustrating and time consuming. A comfortable working environment is just as important when working from home or in a small local office.

Depending on the structure, encourage people working near one another to meet to discuss work. Include home workers and locally based teams in social activities, if possible. Look and listen for any signs of stress. Set out precise procedures on who to contact if things go wrong. Make sure "out of sight" is not "out of mind."

Motivating underperformers

At some stage, you will have to manage someone who is not performing well. For the success of your team and the organization, it is important to deal with their problems because, not only will their performance be affected, but they may also disrupt the motivation of your entire team.

HOW TO... DISCUSS PROBLEMS

Inform the individual in advance what you want to discuss.

↓

State your understanding of the situation.

↓

Let the individual explain how they see the issues.

↓

Get them to accept there is a problem if they have not done so.

↓

Encourage them to come up with some solutions.

↓

Arrange a follow-up meeting.

Identifying problems

Everyone makes mistakes occasionally, and while it is important to respond to them constructively, if you do not deal with underperformance your entire team may lose motivation. Get to know what individual team members are capable of and take action when you notice something is going wrong. Watch out for a change in performance. If someone is making more mistakes than usual, you will need to take some action.

Broaching the subject

How you approach the situation will depend on the circumstances. If someone has made a few silly mistakes you may just need to let them know you have noticed, and ask what happened and how it can be avoided in the future. If problems continue, you will need a more considered meeting. Create the same conditions as you would for a performance appraisal meeting—make sure you have privacy, won't be interrupted, and that the individual is comfortable. Prepare for the meeting, and make sure your facts are correct. Think about the problems and possible reasons for them and, if possible, consider them from the perspective of the individual. Try to remain calm and objective at all times and don't digress by discussing other people or issues that don't affect the individual's own performance.

Finding solutions

There may be deep-seated issues behind the obvious reasons for underperformance, and you need to uncover these, otherwise you will only be applying a temporary patch to the problem. Listen very carefully to what is being said, and then probe gently to get underneath the words. In these situations, people often blame others or find excuses. Make sure they take responsibility for their own performance. For example, if they say problems are occurring because they are consistently receiving information they need too late, ask why they have not spoken to the person causing the delay.

TIP

BE QUICK TO TAKE ACTION
Make sure you deal with performance problems as soon as they occur. It is very easy to ignore them, especially when you are busy, but doing this will not make them go away.

AGREEING TO SOLUTIONS

PROBLEM	RELEVANT QUESTIONS	POSSIBLE SOLUTIONS
Cannot carry out tasks to the required level	Do they have the right training? Do they have the support they need? Were they recruited into the wrong job?	Provide training or equipment; set objectives for improvement; move them to another role; agree that this is not the job for them.
Sudden decline in performance level; making too many silly mistakes	What is causing the lack of concentration? Is it a situation outside work or a problem with a colleague?	Be sympathetic—if necessary let them take some time off. Work together to find a solution.
Slow decline in performance level	Are they bored with their role? Do they need more challenge to motivate them? Are they overwhelmed by work?	Check whether their role can be broadened or shifted. Help them manage their workload better.
Timekeeping is bad	Do they have new commitments at home? Are there any personal issues affecting them?	Give them an option of flexible working hours if it helps. Provide professional help if required.
Relationships with colleagues are poor	Are they overloaded with work? Are they showing signs of stress? Is it because of personality clashes?	Train them in "soft" skills such as emotional intelligence. See if they can be moved to a different team.

Motivating a project team

Cross-departmental project teams are common in many organizations. In this situation, you may well find yourself managing a project involving people who don't report to you. As a project leader, your motivational skills will be critical to the project and your own success.

TIP

ENCOURAGE TEAM SPIRIT

Assist and support other members of the team and do not talk behind their backs.

Maintaining the momentum

Every project goes through stages. At first, everyone is enthusiastic and excited to be involved. Then the work begins. At some stage, problems and setbacks will arise and individuals will become disillusioned and demotivated. This is a critical stage where you, as the project manager, will have to keep the momentum going and make sure people maintain focus and energy. Bring your team together. Remind them that in every project worth doing there are bound to be some setbacks. Bring to mind their earlier successes, explain why the project is still important, and work together to find solutions to the problems. If you still find they are not giving their best to the project, carefully suggest there may be someone better equipped to take their role—they will probably receive your message and change their approach.

Sharing success

Motivating a project team is often one of the most difficult tasks. You may not be the line manager of those involved, so you don't have the usual authority and reward mechanisms at your disposal. You may have been given the opportunity to be the project leader, but you will need to share the success with others. If the other team members see you taking all the credit for the project, they will disengage. You need to manage this balance. If the project is successful, you will get recognized, so be generous with your praise along the way. People like their boss to hear good things about them and it only costs you a little time to copy someone into an email saying thank you. Be careful of individuals who "grandstand" and claim greater responsibility for the success of the project than is justified by their contribution.

TIP

MOTIVATE FOR EVERYONE'S BENEFIT

When motivating your project team, think about what benefits your team can expect from succeeding.

Driving project teams forward

EXUDE ENTHUSIASM
Make the measures of success very explicit and exude your enthusiasm for the project.

GIVE VISIBILITY
Explain that being part of the project will bring people to the notice of their seniors, which can help their careers.

HAVE FUN
Make the project interesting and fun so people participate and contribute willingly.

USE PEER PRESSURE
Involve the whole team to help you apply pressure on any member who is underperforming.

BE FIRM
Threaten to remove an underperforming team member—and make sure you can back up your threat, if necessary.

Motivating teams

Having a group of motivated individuals in your department is a good start, but you won't be really successful unless you have a motivated team. People in teams bounce ideas off of one another and work together to achieve better results than individuals working alone.

Painting a picture of the future

One of the most important motivators for a team is having a common goal each individual has a genuine commitment to achieving. Paint a picture, either graphically or in words, describing what success will look like. Be enthusiastic about achieving it. Talk about your people's role in delivering the success and allude to the benefits of being successful and what success will feel like.

Elements of an effective team

A GOOD LEADER
Having a leader who applies, at team level, all the lessons for motivating each individual on the team.

PEOPLE WHO CAN WORK TOGETHER
Consisting of people who respect fellow team members and are allowed to question and express dissent on occasion.

Creating a sense of belonging

The sense of "belonging" is a very important motivator and, while this does develop naturally when a team has been together over a period of time, a good manager will speed up the process and ensure it is maintained by, for example, celebrating success. Make sure each member of your team knows how they fit into the workings of the whole organization.

Setting benchmarks

At times, seemingly motivated and well-established teams can become complacent. One way of avoiding this is to take your team on benchmarking* visits. Find an organization that does something very well and go and visit them. You will find many organizations are only too happy to do this, particularly if they can "benchmark" with you in return.

*Benchmarking—
the systematic
process of
comparing your
performance
with that of others.

GOOD
COMMUNICATION
PROCESSES
Establishing free-flowing
information within
the team and good
networks and
contacts outside.

OPEN TO
ALTERNATIVES
Considering all
options and opening the
team to external
criticism, or making sure
you have at least one
respected critic on
the team.

COMMON
UNDERSTANDING
Having complete
awareness of the team's
goals along with an
understanding of the
role and contribution
of each team
member.

Bringing it all together

Motivation is part art and part science. You need to understand the theory and apply it in practice with feeling and sincerity. Motivation is like a chain—it is only as strong as its weakest link. It ceases to become effective if any of the links are missing.

GAIN YOUR STAFF'S TRUST
Take genuine interest in your employees. Support them in a professional crisis and look after their long-term career interests to keep them motivated beyond the short term.

Keeping your staff motivated

Motivating people in the short term is relatively easy. But when you have to motivate people over the longer term, enthusiasm alone won't work. To do this you have to create a culture that is conducive to success, balance organizational and personal goals, and ensure people are genuinely interested in the prosperity of the organization. To keep people motivated over the long term, you must be trusted as a leader. You will need to support people by giving them the tools and resources to do the job, helping them overcome obstacles that may get in the way, developing their skills, and rewarding success. Being a good motivator will not only help your organization but will also boost your career, too.

Making each job worthwhile

All jobs in your organization are important—if not, they should be eliminated immediately. Make sure every job is done well, from dealing with customers to producing high-quality products and keeping the facilities clean. Achieving this requires all managers and supervisors in the organization to engage, motivate, and direct their staff. As a manager, it is your responsibility to make the organization a great place for people to work and to encourage them to contribute to the success of the organization.

Tracking performance

Always make sure you and your team are developing, learning, and moving on. You will achieve success only when your team has a positive perception of you, and the organizational environment is favorable and supportive. Use the scorecard featured below to track your performance in motivating people. Think about the elements of the scorecard as the links in a chain. Each link has to be strong to give the chain strength, so use the scorecard as a guide to where you need to focus your attention. It is important that you plan to strengthen any weaknesses that may appear. You could even use the scorecard with trusted team members or colleagues to help you develop your abilities and become a great motivator.

TIP

REVIEW PERFORMANCE

Every six months you should stop and reflect on your team's performance. Ask yourself where you are succeeding, and where you are falling short.

Motivation scorecard

HOW MOTIVATED IS MY STAFF?
Does my team:
• show enthusiasm?
• work well with one another?
• go the extra mile?
• perform well?
• achieve the goals that are set for them?

HOW WELL AM I PERCEIVED?
Do I:
• have the trust of my staff?
• have a good working relationship with my team?
• support my colleagues?
• appear approachable?
• motivate people well?

HOW SUPPORTIVE IS THE ENVIRONMENT?
Do we:
• have the opportunity to do well?
• have the tools to do our job?
• have the support of our bosses and colleagues?

HOW ARE WE LEARNING?
Have I:
• developed my own skills and abilities?
• helped someone learn a new skill in the last month?
• helped someone get promoted this year?

Contents

146 Introduction

CHAPTER 1

Understanding yourself

148 Developing self-awareness

150 Using emotional intelligence

152 Applying assertiveness

154 Examining your assumptions

156 Clarifying your values

158 Developing your personal
mission statement

CHAPTER 2

Interacting with others

160 Communicating effectively

162 Sending messages

164 Listening actively

166 Reading nonverbal cues

168 Teaching skills

170 Giving feedback

172 Negotiating

174 Managing conflict

176 Valuing diversity

CHAPTER 3

Managing a team

178 Setting goals and planning

180 Designing work

182 High-performing teams

186 Delegating effectively

188 Motivating others

192 Appraising performance

CHAPTER 4

Leading others

194 Setting ethical boundaries

196 Ensuring cultural fit

198 Solving problems

200 Building power

202 Managing change

204 Helping others improve

208 Coaching and mentoring

210 Managing careers

Introduction

Managing other people is perhaps the most challenging task facing any manager. It is a dynamic process that is always evolving to accommodate changes in the diverse and complex workplace. *Managing People* provides the understanding and skills that will help you develop and manage effective and high-performing teams of satisfied and productive individuals.

Being an effective manager of people starts with self-awareness and self-management. Interpersonal skills are extremely important, in both one-on-one and team situations—you need to be able to influence others to accomplish their own and the organization's goals. Creating high-performing teams is crucial for any manager today and requires the abilities to set goals, plan and design work, delegate tasks, motivate followers, appraise performance, and solve problems.

As a leader of your team, you need to invest considerable time in helping others improve their performance and develop their careers. Successful mentoring can contribute to fulfillment of personal, professional, and organizational goals. In helping others be successful by applying the skills and guidelines presented in *Managing People*, you will not only enhance your effectiveness as a manager, but also become a leader others want to follow.

Chapter 1

Understanding yourself

Knowing yourself will give you valuable insights into your aptitude for managing others. It allows you to understand how you're perceived by others, why they respond to you in the way they do, and how to get the best from them.

Developing self-awareness

Awareness of your emotions, personality, what you enjoy and dislike, what motivates you, and what comes easily or poses challenges is a key precursor to developing effective managerial ability. Quite simply, if you can't manage yourself, you will not be able to manage anyone else.

Keeping moving

The best way to enhance your self-awareness is to learn in a systematic way from your own experiences. Start by reflecting on situations in your working life, your actions in response to them, and the outcomes of these events. Schedule a regular time to do this, either at the beginning or end of a work day, when you are not in the thick of the action. Give yourself space to reflect, and make sure you can be alone and uninterrupted for a significant period of time. Try to gain a better understanding of what happened and think about how you can learn from each situation.

Keeping a journal

Keeping a journal is a good way to help you learn from experience. Journals are similar to diaries, but include entries that address critical aspects of your managerial experiences and reflect on interactions with bosses, employees, and teammates. Such entries can describe a good (or bad) way someone handled a situation; a problem in the making; the different ways people react to situations; or your thoughts on people in the news, or in books or movies. If you want to solicit feedback, post your journal as an online blog.

TIP

MAKE NOTES

Use your journal to "think on paper" about what you have read about management in this or other books, or your experiences in management training programs.

Analyzing your performance

Assessing your progress toward your goals can help you gain a fuller understanding of your strengths and weaknesses. Whenever you make a key decision or take a key action, write down what you expect will happen. Then, every three or four months, compare the actual results with your expectations. If you practice this method consistently, it will help you discover what you are doing, or failing to do, that deprives you of the full benefits of your strengths, and will demonstrate areas in which you are not particularly competent and cannot perform adequately.

IN FOCUS... FEEDBACK

It is important to find at least one person in your life who will give you honest, gut-level feedback, to help you gain perspective on your experiences and learn from them. This should be someone you trust enough to go to when you have real problems and ask, "Am I off base here? Am I crazy?" This person could be a partner, a mentor, a best friend, a coworker, a therapist, or a personal coach. Today, many organizations are providing their managers with 360-degree feedback, allowing them to receive insights on their strengths and weaknesses from other members of staff.

Using emotional intelligence

Emotional intelligence (EI) is the ability to monitor and work with your and others' emotions. It is measured in EQ, which is the emotional equivalent of IQ. Daniel Goleman—author of the best-selling *Emotional Intelligence*—and other writers suggest that a technically proficient manager with a high EQ will be more successful than a manager who has only a high IQ.

Understanding EQ

Your EQ is the measure of your ability to understand and interact with others and becomes more important the more people you deal with. EQ does not measure personality traits or cognitive capacity. Emotional intelligence can be developed over time and can be improved through training and therapy. Those with a high EQ will be better able to control their own emotions, while at the same time using them as a basis for action. Working with emotions, rather than being at the mercy of them, makes individuals more successful in dealing with the demands of the environment around them. They are better able to control impulses and deal with stress, and better at solving problems. All of these qualities help the individual perform more competently at work.

✔ CHECKLIST APPLYING EMOTIONAL INTELLIGENCE

	YES	NO
• Am I aware of my feelings and do I act accordingly?	☐	☐
• Can I share my feelings in a straightforward, composed manner?	☐	☐
• Do I treat others with compassion, sensitivity, and kindness?	☐	☐
• Am I open to the opinions and ideas of others?	☐	☐
• Can I decisively confront problem people?	☐	☐
• Do I maintain a balance between my personal life and work?	☐	☐

Managing emotions

Emotional intelligence has two aspects: one inward facing and one outward facing. The first of these is your emotional self-awareness and your ability to manage your own emotions. The second is your degree of empathy, or awareness of others' emotions, and your ability to manage relationships with others productively. Both inward- and outward-facing aspects of emotional intelligence are made up of a number of skills or competencies.

Using EI at work

To be a successful manager in today's business world, a high EQ may be more important than sheer intellectual or technical ability. A manager who leads a project team of diverse people will need to understand and interact successfully with others. Applying emotional intelligence at work means you are open to the ideas of others and can build and mend relationships with others. You are aware of your feelings and act accordingly, articulating ideas so others can understand them, developing rapport, building trust, and working toward consensus. Managers who are attuned to their own feelings and the feelings of others use this understanding to enhance personal, team, and organizational performance.

The four competencies of emotional intelligence

SELF-AWARENESS
Emotional self-awareness; accurate self-assessment; self-confidence

SELF-MANAGEMENT
Emotional self-control; trustworthiness; conscientiousness; achievement orientation; adaptability; optimism; initiative

SOCIAL AWARENESS
Empathy; organizational awareness; service orientation

RELATIONSHIP MANAGEMENT
Development of others; inspirational leadership; influence; communication; change catalyst; conflict management; bond building; teamwork and collaboration

Applying assertiveness

An effective manager needs to behave in an active and assertive* manner to get things done. Assertive managers are able to express their feelings and act with appropriate degrees of openness and candor, but still have a regard for the feelings or rights of others.

Understanding personality types

*****Assertive**—being able to make clear statements about what you want from others in a given situation, without being abrasive or demeaning.

Assertiveness and the ability to express your feelings to others are skills people possess to different extents. Some are aggressive, direct, and blunt, and can appear domineering, pushy, or self-centered. Most people tend to be passive, inhibited, and submissive. They bottle up their feelings and fail even to stand up for their legitimate rights. Passive individuals seek to avoid conflicts and tend to sublimate their own needs and feelings in order to satisfy others.

Most people fall between the extremes of passive and aggressive. At these extremes, passive and aggressive behaviors hinder effective managerial relations because neither encourages openness. Effective managers need to be assertive, express their ideas and feelings openly, and stand up for their rights, and all in a way that makes it easier for those they are managing to do the same. The assertive manager is straightforward yet sensitive to the needs of others; he or she does not seek to rule over less assertive people. Seeking dominance may produce short-term results but will not make the best use of the abilities of the team's members.

❓ ASK YOURSELF... AM I ASSERTIVE ENOUGH?

- Does my response accurately reflect how I feel if I'm given a compliment about my work?
- Am I able to speak up when I'm in a group of strangers?
- If others interrupt me when I am speaking, can I hold my ground?
- Do I avoid being taken advantage of by other people?
- Am I able to criticize others' work if I think they might react badly?

Becoming more assertive

STATE YOUR CASE
Try beginning your conversations with "I" phrases, such as "I think," "I believe," or "I need."

BE PREPARED
Prepare for tricky encounters. Have all the facts on hand, and try to anticipate the other person's replies.

USE OPEN QUESTIONS
If you are finding it hard to get a person to talk to you, use open questions that cannot be answered with a simple "yes" or "no" answer.

VISUALIZE YOURSELF
Try assertive role play with a trusted colleague, to help you see yourself as an assertive person.

GET PERSPECTIVE
Try to see a situation from the other person's point of view. Most workplace bullies, for example, are hiding their own insecurities or an inability to do the job. Use this knowledge to give you perspective on any feelings of intimidation or offence you experience, and offer the bully help to overcome their problems.

BE PATIENT
You'll need time and practice to become comfortable with the new behavior. If you are naturally a passive person, recognize that those around you may initially be uncomfortable when you start to become more assertive.

Examining your assumptions

Managers tend to treat their staff according to assumptions they hold about what motivates people. These assumptions create self-fulfilling prophecies in the behavior of the staff. Managers reward what they expect, and consequently only get what they expect. Challenging your own assumptions is one of the first steps in becoming a better manager.

Contrasting X and Y styles

Prominent management theorist Douglas McGregor distinguished two management styles—X and Y—based on the assumptions held by managers about the motives of their staff. X-style managers believe workers need to be coerced and directed. They tend to be strict and controlling, giving their workers little latitude and punishing poor performance. They use few rewards and typically give only negative feedback. These managers see little point in workers having autonomy, because they think the workforce neither expects nor desires cooperation.

X AND Y ASSUMPTIONS

X-STYLE MANAGERS	Y-STYLE MANAGERS
Employees inherently dislike work and will attempt to avoid it.	Employees can enjoy work and can view it as being as natural to them as rest or play.
Employees must be coerced, controlled, or threatened with punishment to achieve goals.	People will exercise self-direction and self-control if they are committed to the objectives behind the tasks they are performing.
Employees will shirk responsibility and seek formal direction.	The average person can learn to accept and seek responsibility.
Most workers place security above all other factors associated with work and will display little ambition.	Most workers place job satisfaction and career fulfillment high on their list of priorities.

Y-style assumptions reflect a much more optimistic view of human nature. Y-style management contends that people will gladly direct themselves toward objectives if their efforts are appropriately rewarded. Managers who hold Y assumptions assume a great deal of confidence in their workers. They are less directive and empower workers, giving them more responsibilities and freedom to accomplish tasks as they deem appropriate. They believe people have hidden potential and the job of the manager is to find and utilize it.

Shaping the environment

Organizations that are designed based on X-style assumptions are very different from those designed by Y-style managers. For example, because they believe their workers are motivated to help the organization reach its goals, Y-style managers will decentralize authority and give more control to workers than will X-style managers. A Y-style manager realizes most people are not resistant to organizational needs by nature, but may have become so as a result of negative experiences, and strives to design structures that involve the employees in executing their work roles, such as participative management and joint goal setting. These approaches allow employees to exercise some self-direction and self-control in their work lives.

In Y-style management, although individuals and groups are still accountable for their activities, the role of the manager is not to exert control but to provide support and advice and to make sure workers have the resources they need to perform their jobs effectively. In contrast, X-style managers consider their role to be to monitor workers to ensure they contribute to the production process and do not threaten product quality.

TIP

ANALYZE YOURSELF

Honestly review every decision you make and every task you delegate. In each case, ask yourself what you assumed the staff involved would think, and how you expected them to behave. Remember that positive expectations help produce positive outcomes.

Clarifying your values

Values are stable and enduring beliefs about what is good, right, and worthwhile and about the behavior that is desirable for achieving what is worthwhile. To be an effective manager, it is necessary to have a good understanding of what your values are and act accordingly.

Defining values

Values are formed early in our lives, from the influence of our parents, teachers, friends, religious leaders, and media role models. Some may change as we go through life and experience different behaviors. Your values manifest themselves in everything you do and the choices you make. If you are someone who particularly values promptness, for example, you will make sure you always behave in ways that mean you are on time for appointments. The thought of being late will stimulate feelings of stress in you, and induce a subsequent adrenaline rush as you hurry to be at the appointment on time. As a manager, it is important for you to clarify your values, so you can determine what your goals are and how you want to manage yourself and others to achieve them.

? ASK YOURSELF... ABOUT YOUR INFLUENCES

- Who are the individuals and what are the events that influenced the development of my value system?
- Are these sources of influence still as important to me as recent events and people who influence me now?
- Are my values still appropriate as guides of behavior in the world I live in today?
- Should I consider changing some of my values to make them more relevant?

Clarifying your personal values

It may sound strange, but one of the best ways to clarify your personal values and gain a clear understanding of what is important to you is to think about how you would like to be remembered in your eulogy. Sit quietly and consider how you want your friends and family to remember you, and what you want your work colleagues to say they thought of you. Also think of your broader contributions—how would you like to be remembered in the communities you are a part of? Make notes, and use the information you write down to identify the values that are most important to you.

Dealing with conflicts

It can be challenging when your personal values conflict with those of your organization, or when there are conflicting values between individuals or subgroups. Value differences can exist, for example, about how to perform jobs, the nature of reward systems, or the degree of intimacy in work relationships. Having a clear understanding of your own personal value set will help you manage these conflict situations. If you are clear about your own values, you can act with integrity and practice what you preach regardless of emotional or social pressure. To address a conflict situation, first make sure you are aware of, understand, and are tolerant of the value differences held by the other parties. This will help you determine whether the value conflict is, in fact, irresolvable and will require personnel changes, or whether compromises and adjustments can be made to accommodate the different perspectives.

IN FOCUS...
TYPES OF VALUE

Values can be classified into two types: terminal and instrumental. Terminal values (your "ends" in life) are desirable ends or goals, such as a comfortable, prosperous life, world peace, great wisdom, or salvation. Instrumental values (the "means" to those ends) are beliefs about what behaviors are appropriate in striving for desired goals and ends. Consider a manager who works extra hours to help deliver a customer's rush order. The attitude displayed is a willingness to help a customer with a problem. The value that serves as the foundation of this attitude might be that of service to others.

Developing your personal mission statement

A personal mission statement provides you with the long-term vision and motivation to manage yourself and others in your team according to your own values. It also allows you to establish your purpose and goals as a manager. Regular evaluation of your performance, based on your mission statement, inspires good self-management.

Defining your future

Your personal mission statement spells out your managerial philosophy. It defines the type of manager you want to be (your character), what you want to accomplish (your contributions), and what principles guide your behavior (your values). It provides you with the vision and values to direct your managerial life—the basis for setting long- and short-term goals, and how best to deploy your time.

TIP

LEARN FROM SETBACKS

Things will not always work out as you have planned. When you experience setbacks, be honest with yourself about what happened and why, and think carefully about whether you need to reevaluate your goals.

Setting out your philosophy

Make sure your personal mission statement is an accurate reflection of your values, goals, and aspirations for success. A personal statement might read: "My career goals are to effectively manage my team to achieve respect and knowledge, to use my talents as a manager to help others, and to play an active role in this organization." Another individual's statement might have a very different focus: "As a manager in this creative firm, I want to establish a fault-free, self-perpetuating learning environment." Reevaluate your mission statement on a regular basis—annually, at least—to ensure it still describes your overall vision for your future as a manager.

BE SMART
Set goals that are Specific, Measurable, Attainable, Realistic, and Time-bound. You are much more likely to achieve goals that are well defined and within your reach.

SET YOUR GOALS
Personalize your goals. You will be far more committed to goals you have set yourself, rather than those that have been set for you by someone else.

SEE THE FUTURE
Develop a vision of what it will be like when you achieve your goals. Your vision of a desirable future can be a powerful motivating force.

Setting and attaining your personal managerial goals

UP

GET SUPPORT
Develop a support group of people who will help you in achieving your goals. Your support group should include those with the resources you need to be successful.

EVALUATE PROGRESS
Continually evaluate your performance against your mission statement. When things do not work out, be honest with yourself about why.

REWARD YOURSELF
Reward yourself for small wins. When you achieve incremental progress toward your goals, treat yourself to a reward, such as a night out or some recreational activity.

Chapter 2

Interacting with others

Your effectiveness as a manager is defined by your ability to interact with other people. A manager needs to guide others through careful communication, teaching, and assessment to work to their full potential, both individually and as a team.

Communicating effectively

It is easy to see investment in communication as a luxury, especially in times of economic adversity. However, good communication is a proven tool for improving commitment in those you are managing, and so for boosting revenue and product quality.

Getting your message across

Communication is the process of sending a message to another person with the intent of evoking an outcome or a change in behavior. It is more efficient when it uses less time and fewer resources; it is effective when the information is conveyed exactly as you intend. Good communication means balancing the two. For example, explaining a new procedure to each staff member individually may be less efficient than calling a meeting where everyone can hear about it. However, if staff members have very disparate sets of interests, one-to-one coaching may be more effective.

Delivering messages

The components of the communication process are the sender, the receiver, the message, and the channel. First, the message is encoded into a format that will get the idea across. Then it is transmitted through the most appropriate channel. This is chosen on the basis of efficiency and effectiveness, as well as practical factors, such as the need to produce a stable record of the communication; whether the information needs to be kept confidential; speed and cost; and the complexity of the communication.

Channels can be oral (speeches, meetings, phone calls, presentations, or informal discussions); written (letters, memoranda, reports, or manuals); electronic (emails, text messages, podcasts, video conferences, websites, or webcasts); or nonverbal (touch, facial expression, or intonation). Finally, the message must be successfully decoded by the receiver. Many factors may intrude, preventing the receiver from correctly understanding what they are told. These range from semantics or different word interpretations to different frames of reference, cultural attitudes, and mistrust.

Before you send a message, ask yourself how much you understand about it, and what is the level of the recipient's understanding? Will the recipient understand the language and jargon you use, and do they have technology that is compatible with yours?

TIP

REDUCE "NOISE"

Noise is anything that interferes, at any stage, with the communication process. The ultimate success of the communication process depends to a large degree on overcoming noise, so make an effort to keep your messages clear, concise, and to the point.

CASE STUDY

Tom's of Maine

Tom Chappell is the founder of Tom's of Maine, a successful natural toothpaste and health company in the US. Chappell is a strong believer in using face-to-face communication to deal with rumors, morale issues, and other communication problems. Every month, he meets informally with his employees and talks about the company's performance and future plans, and solicits feedback from every member of his staff. He says the best way to deal with employee communication is to be honest and forthright, share information, and "tell it like it is."

Sending messages

Effective communication with those you are managing requires that you send clear and comprehensible messages that will be understood as you intend them to be. You can transmit messages more effectively by making them clearer and developing your credibility.

TIP

BE CONSISTENT
Ensure your messages are congruent with your actions. Saying one thing and doing another is confusing and creates distrust.

Getting your point across

To be successful, every manager must develop the ability to send clear, unambiguous messages that efficiently convey the information they want to deliver. Effective messages use multiple channels to get the information across. For example, if you match your facial and body gestures to the intended meaning of a message while drawing a diagram to explain it, you are using three channels. Make sure you take responsibility for the feelings and evaluations in your messages, using personal pronouns such as "I" and "mine." Make the information in your messages specific, and refer to concrete details, to avoid the possibility of misinterpretation. Keep your language simple, and avoid technical jargon.

Hitting the right tone

"I need the report delivered by 4:30 on Friday afternoon."

"I'm not happy when you're late for meetings."

"I need the report delivered as soon as possible."

"Everyone feels you're not pulling your weight."

CHECKLIST COMMUNICATING USING EFFECTIVE MESSAGES

	YES	NO
• Do I use multiple channels when sending messages?	☐	☐
• Do I provide all relevant information?	☐	☐
• Am I complete and specific?	☐	☐
• Do I use "I" statements to claim my messages as my own?	☐	☐
• Am I congruent in my verbal and nonverbal messages?	☐	☐
• Do I use language the receiver can understand?	☐	☐
• Do I obtain feedback to ensure my message has been understood and not misinterpreted?	☐	☐

Being credible

Sender credibility is reflected in the recipient's belief that the sender is trustworthy. To increase your sender credibility, make sure you:

• Know what you are talking about: recipients are more attentive when they perceive that senders have expertise.

• Establish mutual trust: owning up to your motives can eliminate the recipient's anxiety about your intentions.

• Share all relevant information: senders are seen as unethical when they intentionally provoke receivers into doing things they would not have done if they had had all of the information.

• Be honest: one of the key things people want in a leader and coworker is honesty. As a sender, avoid any form of deception, which is the conscious alteration of information to influence another's perceptions.

• Be reliable: if you are dependable, predictable, and consistent, recipients will perceive you as being trustworthy.

• Be warm, friendly, and supportive: this will give you more personal credibility than a posture of hostility, arrogance, or abruptness.

• Be dynamic: being confident, dynamic, and positive in your delivery of information will make you seem more credible than someone who is passive, withdrawn, and unsure.

• Make appropriate self-disclosures: responsibly revealing your feelings, reactions, needs, and desires to others is essential when establishing supportive relationships. It facilitates congruency, builds trust and credibility, and helps recipients of your messages develop empathy and understanding with you.

Listening actively

Many communication problems develop because listening skills are ignored, forgotten, or taken for granted. Active listening is making sense of what you hear. It requires paying attention and interpreting all verbal, visual, and vocal stimuli presented to you.

Understanding the basics

Active listening has four essential ingredients: concentration, empathy, acceptance, and taking responsibility for completely understanding the message. To listen actively, you must concentrate intensely on what the speaker is saying and tune out competing miscellaneous thoughts that create distractions. Try to understand what the speaker

LISTENING WELL

FAST TRACK	**OFF TRACK**
Keeping an open mind, free from preconceived ideas	Judging the value of the speaker's ideas by appearance and delivery
Giving the speaker your full attention while they are talking	Thinking about what you are going to say while the speaker is talking
Assessing the full meaning behind the words that are being spoken	Listening for specific facts rather than the overall message
Asking questions when you need more information	Interrupting the speaker when you have a better idea
Withholding judgment until the speaker has finished speaking	Always trying to have the last word

wants to communicate rather than what you want to understand. Listen objectively and resist the urge to start evaluating what the person is saying, or you may miss the rest of the message. Finally, do whatever is necessary to get the full, intended meaning from the speaker's message—listen for feelings and content, and ask questions to make sure you have understood.

Employing the techniques

Active listening is hard work and starts with your own personal motivation. If you are unwilling to exert the effort to hear and understand, no amount of additional advice is going to improve your listening effectiveness. If you are motivated to become an effective listener, there are a number of specific techniques you can use to improve your skills:
• Make eye contact: this focuses your attention, reduces the likelihood you will become distracted, and encourages the speaker.
• Show interest: use nonverbal signals, such as head nods, to convey to the speaker you're listening.
• Avoid distracting actions: looking at your watch or shuffling papers are signs you aren't fully attentive and might be missing part of the message.
• Take in the whole picture: interpret feelings and emotions as well as factual content.
• Ask questions: seek clarification if you don't understand something. This also reassures the speaker you're listening to them.
• Paraphrase: restate what the speaker has said in your own words with phrases such as "What I hear you saying is…" or "Do you mean…?"
• Don't interrupt: let speakers complete their thoughts before you try to respond.
• Confront your biases: use information about speakers to improve your understanding of what they are saying, but don't let your biases distort the message.

SET THE CONTEXT

Mentally summarize and integrate what a speaker says, and put each new bit of information into the context of what has preceded it.

Reading nonverbal cues

Nonverbal communication is made up of visual, vocal, and tactile signals and the use of time, space, and image. As much as 93 percent of the meaning transmitted in face-to-face communication can come from nonverbal channels, so you should be aware of these cues.

Decoding the truth

The visual part of nonverbal communication is often called body language. It includes expressions, eye movement, posture, and gestures. The face is the best communicator of nonverbal messages. By "reading" a person's facial expression, we can detect unvocalized feelings. Appearance is important, too—people do judge a book by its cover, and most of us react favorably to an expected image. In terms of dress, color can convey meaning (brown can convey trust; dark colors, power), as does style (pure fibers such as wool or silk suggest higher status). Posture is important—a relaxed posture, such as sitting back with legs stretched out and hands behind the head, signals confidence.

If a person says one thing but communicates something different through intonation and body language, tension and distrust can arise; the receiver will typically choose the nonverbal interpretation because it is more reliable than the verbal. For example, if you ask your boss when you will be eligible for a promotion and she looks out of the window, covers a yawn, and says, "I would say you might have a chance in the not-too-distant future," you should not count on being promoted soon.

NERVOUSNESS
Clearing one's throat, covering the mouth while speaking, fidgeting, shifting weight from one foot to the other, tapping fingers, pacing.

BOREDOM OR IMPATIENCE
Drumming fingers, foot swinging, brushing or picking at lint, doodling, or looking at one's watch.

Feelings that can be read from gestures and body language

OPENNESS
Holding hands in an open position, having an unbuttoned coat or collar, removing one's coat, moving closer, leaning slightly forward, and uncrossing arms and legs.

DEFENSIVENESS
Holding body rigid, with arms or legs tightly crossed, eyes glancing sideways, minimal eye contact, lips pursed, fists clenched, and a downcast head.

CONFIDENCE, SUPERIORITY, AND AUTHORITY
Using relaxed and expansive gestures, such as leaning back with fingers laced behind the head and hands together at the back with chin thrust upward.

Teaching skills

As a manager, an important part of your role is to help those you are managing develop their skills. If you can encourage the development of skills such as self-awareness, communication, and time management, you will be rewarded with a high-performing team.

HOW TO... TEACH NEW SKILLS

Help the learner form a conceptual understanding of a new skill.

↓

Plan how they can test their understanding of the skill.

↓

Get the learner to apply the new skill in concrete experience.

↓

Observe what happened and discuss ways in which they can improve.

Learning by experience

People learn faster and retain more information if they have to exert some kind of active effort. The famous quote, attributed to Confucius: "I hear and I forget. I see and I remember. I do and I understand" is frequently used to support the value of learning through experience. A major implication of this notion is that new skills can be learned only through experimenting with new behaviors, observing the results, and learning from the experience. The learning of new skills is maximized when learners get the opportunity to combine watching, thinking, and doing. The experiential learning model encompasses four elements: learning new concepts (conceptualizing); planning how to test the ideas (plan to test); actively applying the skill in a new experience (gaining concrete experience); and examination of the consequences of the experience (reflective observation). After reflecting on the experience, the learner uses the lessons they have learned from what happened to create a refined conceptual map of the skill, and the cycle continues.

To use the experiential learning model to teach skills, you need to: make sure the learner understands the skill both conceptually and behaviorally; give them opportunities to practice it; give feedback on how well they are performing the skill; and encourage them to use the skill often enough so that it becomes integrated into their behavioral repertoire.

EFFECTIVE APPROACHES TO TEACHING SKILLS

APPROACH	WHY IT WORKS
Being prepared Knowing ahead of time what you want the outcome of your skills training to be.	Unless you know where you want things to go, you won't know how to conduct yourself to get there.
Listening Keeping communication lines open and indicating to others that their opinions are important.	The key to effectively teaching a skill is often expressed by the learner, but overlooked by the manager when they fail to hear it.
Using questions Presenting a concept, options for applying it, and the consequences, then asking the learner what they will do.	Asking rather than telling an employee how best to apply a new skill shows respect and, because it allows them to think it through for themselves, it helps them learn faster.
Being positive Correcting mistakes in a positive way, not in one that is patronizing or makes others feel worthless and inferior.	Using positive messages, such as "I can see you want to do well and I think I can help you learn to do better," will help motivate the person you are teaching.
Being honest and upfront Making it clear to the learner what is really required of them, and why this is important.	People will be more willing to accept your skill teaching if they trust and respect you because they will believe you are honest and forthright.
Setting performance targets Indicating the acceptable level of performance you expect from those you are teaching, and holding them to it.	In the long run, people will respect you more if you hold them to a standard of performance because they will know any praise they receive from you is sincere and deserved.

Inspiring others

When you endeavor to teach new skills to others, you are attempting to motivate specific behavior changes in them. This is more effective if you can convince those you are teaching that, by acting as you suggest, they will gain something they value. Successful teaching requires you to inspire others to want to cooperate with you. However, different people consider different skills to be more or less valuable to them, so you will also discover that the majority of responsibility for the learning of a new skill rests with the person you are teaching. Learners who really want to improve their skills and are willing to put in the effort will be successful.

Giving feedback

Most managers will enthusiastically give their employees positive feedback but often avoid or delay giving negative feedback, or substantially distort it, for fear of provoking a defensive reaction. However, improving employees' performance depends on balanced and considered feedback.

Valuing feedback

Providing regular feedback to your employees will improve their performance. This is because:
• Feedback can induce a person to set goals, which act as motivators of their performance.
• Feedback tells the person how well they are progressing toward those goals. Positive feedback gives reinforcement, while constructive negative feedback can result in increased effort.
• The content of the feedback will suggest ways the person can improve their performance.
• Providing feedback demonstrates to a person that you care about how they are doing.

   As a rule, positive feedback is usually accepted readily, while negative feedback often meets resistance. When preparing to deliver negative feedback, first make sure you are aware of any conflict that could arise and think about how to deal with it. Be sure that negative feedback comes from a credible source, that it is objective, and that it is supported by hard data such as quantitative performance indicators and specific examples.

TALK ABOUT THE JOB
Keep feedback job-related. Never make personal judgments, such as "You are stupid and incompetent."

GIVE DETAIL
Avoid vague statements such as "You have a bad attitude" or "I'm impressed with the job you did." The recipient needs to understand exactly what they have or haven't done well.

How to provide feedback

USE GOALS
Keep feedback goal-oriented. Its purpose is not to unload your feelings on someone.

BE NONJUDGMENTAL
Keep feedback descriptive and fair rather than judgmental.

MAKE IT ATTAINABLE
When delivering negative feedback, make sure you only criticize shortcomings over which the person has some control.

EXPLAIN YOUR REASONS
Explain to the recipient why you are being critical or complimentary about specific aspects of their performance.

ENSURE A GOOD FIT
Tailor the feedback to fit the person. Consider past performance and future potential in designing the frequency, amount, and content of performance feedback.

CHECK UNDERSTANDING
Once you have given your feedback, have the recipient rephrase the content to check they have fully understood what you have said and are taking away the right message from your feedback session.

Negotiating

Negotiation is a process by which two or more parties exchange goods or services and attempt to agree on the exchange rate for them. Managers spend a lot of time negotiating, and need to be able to do it well. They have to negotiate salaries for incoming employees, cut deals with superiors, bargain over budgets, work out differences with associates, and resolve conflicts between members of their team.

Understanding approaches

There are two general approaches to negotiation: distributive and integrative bargaining. Distributive bargaining assumes zero-sum conditions, that is: "Any gain I make is at your expense" and vice versa. Integrative bargaining assumes a win–win solution is possible. Each is appropriate in different situations.

Distributive bargaining tactics focus on getting an opponent to agree to a deal that meets your specific goals. Such tactics include persuading opponents of the impossibility of getting their needs met in other ways or the advisability of accepting your offer; arguing that your position is fair, while theirs is not; and trying to get the other party to feel emotionally generous toward you and accept an outcome that meets your goals.

CASE STUDY

A win–win solution

After closing a $15,000 order from a small clothing retailer, sales rep Deb Hansen called in the order to her firm's credit department and was told the firm could not approve credit for this customer because of a past slow-pay record. The next day, Deb and the firm's credit supervisor met to discuss the problem. Deb did not want to lose the business; neither did the credit supervisor, but he also didn't want to get stuck with a bad debt. The two openly reviewed their options. After considerable discussion, they agreed on a solution: the credit supervisor would approve the sale, but the clothing store's owner would provide a bank guarantee that would assure payment if the bill was not paid within 60 days.

Finding solutions

Integrative, or win–win, bargaining is generally preferable to distributive bargaining. Distributive bargaining leaves one party a loser, and so it tends to build animosities and deepen divisions between people. On the other hand, integrative bargaining builds long-term relationships and facilitates working together in the future. It bonds negotiators and allows each to leave the bargaining table feeling that he or she has achieved a victory. For integrative bargaining to work, however, both parties must openly share all information, be sensitive to each other's needs, trust each other, and remain flexible.

Negotiating well

Careful attention to a few key guidelines can increase a manager's odds of successful negotiation outcomes. Always start by considering the other party's point of view. Acquire as much information as you can about their interests and goals. Always go into a negotiation with a concrete strategy. Treat negotiations the way expert players treat the game of chess, always knowing ahead of time how they will respond to any given situation.

HOW TO... NEGOTIATE

Begin with a positive overture, and establish rapport and mutual interests.

↓

Make a small concession early on if you can. Concessions tend to be reciprocated and can lead to a quick agreement.

↓

Concentrate on the issues, not on the personal characteristics or personality of your opponent.

↓

If your opponent attacks you or gets emotional, let them blow off steam without taking it personally.

↓

Pay little attention to initial offers, treating them merely as starting points.

↓

Focus on the other person's interests and your own goals and principles while you generate other possibilities.

↓

Emphasize win–win solutions to the negotiation.

↓

Make your decisions based on principles and results, not emotions or pressure.

Managing conflict

Conflict is natural to organizations and can never be completely eliminated. If not managed properly, conflict can be dysfunctional and lead to undesirable consequences, such as hostility, lack of cooperation, and even violence. When managed effectively, conflict can stimulate creativity, innovation, and change.

TIP

PUT YOURSELF IN THEIR SHOES

Empathize with the other parties in the conflict, and try to understand their values, personality, feelings, and resources. Make sure you know what is at stake for them.

Understanding the causes

Conflicts exist whenever an action by one party is perceived as preventing or interfering with the goals, needs, or actions of another party. Conflicts have varying causes but are generally rooted in one of three areas: problems in communication; disagreements over work design, policies, and practices; and personal differences.

Disagreements frequently arise from semantic difficulties, misunderstandings, poor listening, and noise in the communication channels. Communication breakdowns are inevitable in work settings, often causing workers to focus on placing blame on others instead of trying to solve problems.

Conflicts can also result when people or groups disagree over goal priorities, decision alternatives, performance criteria, and resource allocations. The things people want, such as promotions, wage increases, and office space, are scarce resources that must be divided up. Ambiguous rules, regulations, and performance standards can also create conflicts.

Individual idiosyncrasies and differences in personal value systems originating from different cultural backgrounds, education, experience, and training often lead to conflicts. Stereotyping, prejudice, ignorance, and misunderstanding may cause people who are different to be perceived by some to be untrustworthy adversaries.

Handling conflict

There are five basic approaches managers can use to try to resolve conflicts. Each has strengths and weaknesses, so choose the one most appropriate to your situation:

• Avoidance: not every conflict requires an assertive action. Avoidance works well for trivial conflicts or if emotions are running high and opposing parties need time to cool down.

• Accommodation: if you need to maintain a harmonious relationship, you may choose to concede your position on an issue that is much more important to the other party.

• Competition: satisfying your own needs at the expense of other parties is appropriate when you need a quick resolution on important issues, or where an unpopular action must be taken.

• Compromise: this works well when the parties are equal in power, or when you need a quick solution or a temporary solution to a complex issue.

• Collaboration: use this when the interests of all parties are too important to be ignored. Discuss the issues openly and honestly with all parties, listen actively, and make a careful deliberation over a full range of alternatives.

Approaches to conflict-handling

	UNCOOPERATIVE	COOPERATIVE
ASSERTIVE	**COMPETITION** Using your formal authority to resolve issues the way you want.	**COLLABORATION** Finding a solution that is advantageous to all parties.
	COMPROMISE Each party gives up something to reach a solution that is satisfactory to all.	
UNASSERTIVE	**AVOIDANCE** Withdrawing or postponing the conflict.	**ACCOMMODATION** Yielding to another party's position.

Valuing diversity

Understanding and managing people who are similar to us can be challenging, but understanding and managing those who are dissimilar from us and from each other is tougher. As the workplace becomes more diverse and as business becomes more global, managers must understand how cultural diversity affects the expectations and behavior of everyone in the organization.

TIP

LET EVERYONE KNOW

Make a public commitment to valuing diversity. This will ensure that you are accountable for your actions and may attract potential employees who prefer to work for someone who values equal opportunities for all.

Understanding the changes

The labor market is dramatically changing. Most countries are experiencing an increase in the age of their workforce, increased immigration, and, in many, a rapid increase in the number of working women. The globalization of business also brings with it a cross-cultural mandate. With more businesses selling and manufacturing products and services abroad, managers increasingly see the need to ensure their employees can relate to customers from many different cultures. Rich McGinn, of US telecommunications giant Lucent Technologies, said: "We are in a war for talent. And the only way you can meet your business imperatives is to have all people as part of your talent pool." Workers who believe their differences are not merely tolerated but valued by their employer are more likely to be loyal, productive, and committed.

Capitalizing on diversity

Managers face many challenges capitalizing on diversity, such as coping with employees' unfamiliarity with native languages, learning which rewards are valued by different ethnic groups, and providing career development programs that fit the values of different ethnic groups. There are several ways for you to try to capitalize on diversity:

• Communicate your objectives and expectations about diversity to employees through a range of channels, such as vision and mission statements, value statements, slogans, creeds, newsletters, speeches, emails, and everyday conversations.

• Recruit through nontraditional sources. Relying on current employee referrals usually produces a limited range of candidates. Try instead to identify novel sources for recruitment, such as women's job networks, ethnic newspapers, training centers for the disabled, urban job banks, and over-50s clubs.

• Use diverse incentives for motivation. Most studies on motivation are by North American researchers on North American workers. Consequently, these studies are based on beliefs that most people work to promote their own well-being and get ahead. This may be at odds with people from more collectivist countries, such as Venezuela, Singapore, Japan, and Mexico, where individuals are driven by their loyalty to the organization or society, not their own self-interest.

TIP

PRACTICE WHAT YOU PREACH

First look into your heart and mind and root out any prejudice. Then, demonstrate your acceptance in everything you say and do.

Chapter 3

Managing a team

Teams are the cornerstones of most public and nonprofit organizations. Successful team leaders understand what makes a team effective and what can lead to failure. To be a successful manager, you need to be able to plan and design the work of your team, delegate tasks effectively, monitor progress, and motivate your team to excel.

Setting goals and planning

Planning is a key skill for any manager and starts with having a good understanding of the organization's objectives. It involves establishing a strategy for achieving those goals using the personnel available, and developing the means to integrate and coordinate necessary activities.

Knowing your goals

Planning is concerned with ends (what needs to be done) and means (how those ends are to be achieved). In order to create a plan, managers must first identify the organization's goals—what it is trying to achieve. Goals are the foundation of all other planning activities. They refer to the desired outcomes for the entire organization, for groups and teams within the organization, and for individuals. Goals provide the direction for all management decisions and form the criteria against which actual accomplishments can be measured.

Setting your goals

There are five basic rules that can help you set effective goals. Always make your goals SMART: Specific, Measurable, Aligned, Reachable, and Time-bound.

• **Specific** Goals are meaningful only when they are specific enough to be measured and verified.

• **Measurable** Goals need to have a clear outcome that can be objectively assessed. They also need to have clear benchmarks that can be checked along the way.

• **Aligned** Goals should contribute to the mission, vision, and strategic plan of the organization and be congruent with the values and objectives of the employee implementing them.

• **Reachable** Goals should require you to stretch to reach them, but not be set unrealistically high.

• **Time-bound** Open-ended goals can be neglected because there is no sense of urgency to complete them. Whenever possible, goals should include a specific time limit for accomplishment.

HOW TO... DEVELOP AND IMPLEMENT A PLAN

Define your overall goals by asking questions such as "Why do we exist?" and "What do we do?"

▼

Thoroughly analyze your working environment to identify opportunities you can exploit and threats you may encounter.

▼

Use the results to set objectives you want to meet. These will create a standard against which to measure your progress.

▼

Formulate a plan to achieve those objectives—what needs to be done, by whom, and by when.

▼

Implement the plan, clarifying roles and providing support.

▼

Monitor your progress to make sure you are on the right track.

TIP

LOOK TO THE FUTURE

Write down three SMART goals you want your team to achieve in the next five years, and then plan how you will reach them.

Designing work

Job design refers to the way tasks are combined to form complete jobs. It involves trying to shape the right jobs to conform to the right people, taking into account both the organization's goals and the employees' satisfaction. Well-designed jobs lead to high motivation, high-quality performance, high satisfaction, and low absenteeism and turnover.

TIP

GET THE RIGHT PERSON FOR THE JOB

It is very difficult to change how a person performs completely, so try to match people to jobs they are good at. This will make them most likely to achieve good results.

Defining jobs

Jobs vary considerably. A lifeguard, for example, will have very different day-to-day responsibilities from an accountant or a construction worker. But any job can be described in terms of five core job dimensions:

• Skill variety: the degree to which a job requires a variety of different activities so the worker can employ a number of different skills and talents.

• Task identity: the degree to which a job requires completion of a whole and identifiable piece of work.

• Task significance: the degree to which a job has an impact on the lives of other people.

• Autonomy: the degree to which a job provides freedom and discretion to the worker in scheduling their tasks and in determining how the work will be carried out.

• Feedback: the degree to which the worker gets direct and clear information about the effectiveness of his or her performance.

As a manager, you can maximize your team's performance by enhancing these five dimensions. Skill variety, task identity, and task significance combine to create meaningful work. Jobs with these characteristics will be perceived as important, valuable, and worthwhile. Jobs that possess autonomy give workers a sense of responsibility for their results. Jobs that provide feedback indicate to the employee how effectively he or she is performing.

Ways to design work by enhancing the five dimensions

1 COMBINE TASKS
Put existing fragmented tasks together to form larger modules of work. This can help increase skill variety and task identity.

2 CREATE NATURAL WORK UNITS
Design tasks to form an identifiable whole to increase employee "ownership" and encourage workers to view their jobs as important.

3 ESTABLISH CLIENT RELATIONSHIPS
Building direct relationships between the worker and the client—the user of the product or the service the employee works on—increases skill variety, autonomy, and feedback.

4 EXPAND JOBS VERTICALLY
Giving employees responsibilities formerly reserved for managers closes the gap between the "doing" and "controlling" aspects of the job and increases autonomy.

5 IMPROVE FEEDBACK CHANNELS
Feedback tells employees how well they are performing, and whether their performance is improving, deteriorating, or remaining constant. Employees should receive feedback directly as they do their jobs.

High-performing teams

As Lee Iacocca, former CEO of Chrysler Corporation, said: "All business operations can be reduced to three words: people, product, and profit. People come first. Unless you've got a good team, you can't do much with the other two." Successful managers are those who create, work with, and manage successful teams.

Defining high-performing teams

A team is two or more people who meet regularly, perceive themselves as a distinct entity distinguishable from others, have complementary skills, and are committed to a common purpose, a set of performance goals, and an approach for which they hold themselves mutually accountable. High-performing teams engage in collective work produced by coordinated joint efforts that result in more than the sum of the individual efforts. Teams of 10 or fewer members find it easiest to interact constructively and reach agreement.

Understanding team performance

WHO ARE WE?
Sharing strengths, weaknesses, work preferences, and values allows the establishment of a set of common beliefs for the team, creating a group identity and a feeling of "what we stand for."

WHERE ARE WE NOW?
Understanding the current position means a team can reinforce its strengths, improve on its weaknesses, and identify opportunities to capitalize on and threats to be aware of.

WHERE ARE WE GOING?
Teams need to have a vision of the pot of gold at the end of the rainbow. They also need a mission, a purpose, and a set of specific team goals they are all excited about.

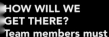

**HOW WILL WE
GET THERE?**
Team members must
understand who will
do what and when to
accomplish team goals,
and must be clear about
their job description,
roles on the team,
responsibilities, and
areas of authority

**WHAT SUPPORT DO
WE GET/NEED?**
Reviewing each
member's training and
development needs
can set the stage for
individual training,
counseling, and
mentoring, which will
strengthen both the
individual and the team.

**HOW EFFECTIVE
ARE WE?**
Regular performance
reviews of quantity
and quality outputs and
the team process—
with recognition and
reward for success—
ensure achievement
of team goals and
provide members

IN FOCUS... MUTUAL TRUST

A climate of mutual trust is essential in a high-performing team—each member of the team needs to know they can depend on the others. Successful managers build mutual trust by creating a climate of openness in which employees are free to discuss problems without fear of retaliation. They are approachable, respectful, and listen to team members' ideas, and develop a reputation for being fair, objective, and impartial in their treatment of others. Consistency and honesty are key, so they avoid erratic and unpredictable behavior and always follow through on any explicit and implied promises they make. Communication is at the heart of building and maintaining mutual interdependence between members of a team. Managers of high-performing teams keep team members informed about upper-management decisions and policies and give accurate feedback on their performance. They are also open and candid about their own problems and limitations.

TIP

CHANGE PERSONNEL

If your teams get bogged down in their own inertia or internal fighting, rotate the members. Consider how certain personalities will mesh and re-form your teams in ways that will better complement skills.

Achieving good teamwork

To help your teams perform to the best of their ability, create clear goals. All team members need to have a thorough understanding of the goals of the team and a belief that these goals embody a worthwhile result. This encourages team members to sublimate personal concerns to those of the team. Members need to be committed to the team's goals, know what they are expected to accomplish, and understand how they will work together to achieve these goals.

However, these goals must be attainable; team members can lose morale if it seems they are not. To avoid this, set smaller interim milestones in the path to your overall goal. As these smaller goals are attained, your team's success is reinforced. Cohesiveness is increased, morale improves, and confidence builds.

As the manager of a team, it is your job to provide the resources and support the members need to achieve success. Offer skills training where needed, either personally or by calling in specialists within your organization or outside training services.

Steering your team

Team members should all share in the glory when their team succeeds, and they should share in the blame when it fails. However, members need to know they cannot ride on the backs of others. Identify what each member's individual contribution to the team's work should be and make it a part of his or her overall performance appraisal.

To help monitor performance, select members of the team to act as participant–observers. While a team is working, the role of the participant–observer is to focus on the processes being used: the sequence of actions that takes place between team members to achieve the team's goal. Periodically, the participant–observer should stop the team from working on its task and discuss the process members are engaged in. The objectives of the participant–observer are to continuously improve the team's functioning by discussing the processes being used and creating strategies for improving them.

Setting standards

Create a performance agreement to record the details of what the team is aiming to achieve, what is required and expected of every team member, and what support will be available to them. Setting out the framework for team success clearly helps ensure there is a mutual understanding and common vision of the desired results and emphasizes the standards you expect from every team member.

CHECKLIST CREATING A TEAM PERFORMANCE AGREEMENT

	YES	NO
• Have I identified what is to be done and when?	☐	☐
• Have I specified the boundaries (guiding rules of behavior) or the means for accomplishing results?	☐	☐
• Have I identified the human, financial, technical, or organizational support available to help achieve the results?	☐	☐
• Have I established the standards of performance and the time intervals for evaluation?	☐	☐
• Have I specified what will happen in performance evaluations and the consequences of not meeting the standards?	☐	☐

Delegating effectively

Managers are responsible for getting things done through other people. You need to accomplish assigned goals by delegating responsibility and authority to others. Empowering others through delegation is one of the most powerful managerial tools for increasing productivity.

Empowering others

Managers delegate by transferring authority and responsibility for work to employees. Delegation empowers employees to achieve goals by allowing them to make their own decisions about how to do a job. Delegation also helps develop employees for promotion opportunities by expanding their knowledge, job capabilities, and decision-making skills. Delegation is frequently depicted as having four key components:

- **Allocation of duties** Before a manager can delegate authority, the tasks and activities that need to be accomplished must be explained.
- **Delegation of authority** Delegation is the process of transferring authority to empower a subordinate to act for you as a manager.
- **Assignment of responsibility** Managers should assign responsibility to the empowered employee for performing the job adequately.
- **Creation of accountability** Managers should hold empowered employees responsible for properly carrying out their duties. This includes taking responsibility for the completion of tasks assigned to them and also being accountable to the manager for the satisfactory performance of that work.

Feeling the benefits

Effective delegation is key for any manager. It will free up your time, allowing you to focus on big-picture strategic activities. It can also lead to better decision-making, because it pushes decisions down the organization, meaning that decision-makers are often closer to the problems. It also helps those you are managing develop their own decision-making skills and prepares them for future promotion opportunities.

Letting go

Managers often have trouble delegating. Some are afraid to give up control, explaining, "I like to do things myself, because then I know it's done and it's done right." Others lack confidence in their employees or fear they may be criticized for others' mistakes. While you may be capable of doing the tasks you delegate better, faster, or with fewer mistakes, it is not possible to do everything yourself. However, you should expect, and accept, some mistakes by those you delegate to. Mistakes are often good learning experiences. You also should put adequate controls and mechanisms for feedback in place so you will know what is happening.

HOW TO...
DELEGATE

CLARIFY THE ASSIGNMENT
Explain what is being delegated, the results you expect, and the timeframe.

↓

SET BOUNDARIES
Make sure the delegatees understand precisely what the parameters are of the authority you are bestowing on them.

↓

ENCOURAGE PARTICIPATION
Involve delegatees in decisions about what is delegated, how much authority is needed, and standards to be attained.

↓

INFORM OTHERS
Let everyone who may be affected know what has been delegated to whom and how much authority has been granted.

↓

ESTABLISH CONTROLS
Agree on a specific time for completion of the task, and set dates when progress will be checked and problems discussed.

↓

ENCOURAGE DEVELOPMENT
Insist from the beginning that when delegatees come to you with a problem, they also bring a possible solution.

Motivating others

Every day, people make decisions about how much effort to put into their work. Managers have many opportunities to influence these decisions and motivate their team by providing challenging work, recognizing outstanding performance, allowing participation in decisions that affect employees, and showing concern for personal issues.

Understanding needs

As a manager, you need to understand what drives your team to do the best that they can. American psychologist Abraham Maslow proposed that every individual has a five-level hierarchy of needs they are driven to attempt to satisfy. Once a lower-level need has been largely satisfied, its impact on a person's behavior diminishes, and they begin to be motivated to gain the next highest level need.

There are two aspects to what makes a person perform well: ability and motivation. Ability is the product of aptitude, training, and resources, while motivation is the product of desire and commitment. All of these elements are required for high performance levels. If someone is not performing

CASE STUDY

Prioritizing needs

Theresa, a successful technical writer and a single parent, had been earning a good salary and benefits that enabled her to provide for her family's physical well-being: ample food, comfortable housing and clothing, and good medical care. Her company then announced it was downsizing, and she feared being laid off. This triggered concerns about her safety needs and meant she became much less concerned about the higher-order needs of belonging to a group or her own self-esteem to perform creative and technically accurate work. Instead, she was motivated to do whatever was necessary to make sure she kept her job or could find a new one. Once Theresa knew her job was safe, she changed back to having a higher-order need, energizing her behavior.

well, the first question you should ask yourself is:
"Is their poor performance the result of a lack of
ability or a lack of motivation?" Motivational
methods can often be very effective for improving
performance, but if the problem is lack of ability,
no amount of pressure or encouragement will help.
What the person needs is training, additional
resources, or a different job.

Maslow's hierarchy of needs

**SELF-
ACTUALIZATION
NEEDS**
The highest level is to
feel we are achieving life
goals. At work, this means
being able to exercise
creativity and develop and fully
utilize our skills.

ESTEEM NEEDS
Next, we are motivated by the need for
self-esteem and esteem from others, such as
recognition for accomplishments and promotion.

SOCIAL NEEDS
Once you feel reasonably secure, social needs begin
to take over. At work, this means having good relationships
with coworkers and participating in company social functions.

SAFETY NEEDS
Once physiological needs are satisfied, safety needs are aroused.
These can be satisfied at work by having job security and safe working
conditions, and receiving medical benefits.

PHYSIOLOGICAL NEEDS
Our most basic needs are for physical survival, such as to satisfy hunger or thirst.
At work, this is receiving enough pay to buy food and clothing and pay the rent.

Using positive reinforcement

Rewarding progress and success and recognizing achievements are powerful ways to motivate your team. By rewarding someone for doing something right, you positively reinforce that behavior, giving them an incentive for doing it again. There are two basic types of reward: extrinsic and intrinsic. Many people depend on and highly value extrinsic rewards, which are externally bestowed, such as praise, a promotion, or a pay raise. Others place a high value on intrinsic rewards, which originate from their own personal feelings about how they performed or the satisfaction that they derive from a job well done.

Rewarding success

Try to understand whether each individual you are managing values intrinsic or extrinsic rewards more highly. If you always praise achievements, for example, a motivated person who excels largely for the feelings of intrinsic satisfaction will probably begin to view you as superficial. The professional may think, "I know I did a superb job on this project. Why is my manager being so condescending?"

People also desire different types of extrinsic rewards. Praise may be perfectly acceptable to the person motivated by affiliation and relationship needs, but may do nothing for the person expecting a more tangible reward, like money. Typical extrinsic rewards are favorable assignments, trips to desirable destinations, tuition reimbursement, pay raises, bonuses, promotions, and office placements.

**? ASK YOURSELF...
CAN I DRAW ON
MY EXPERIENCE?**

- Can you think of a coach, teacher, or manager who motivated you to enhance your performance in a particular task?
- What did they do to motivate you?
- How did you feel as a result of their actions?
- Can you recreate their actions or use their approach when trying to motivate your team?

Motivating your team

There are other methods of motivating employees in addition to direct positive reinforcement. These include:

Strengthening effort–performance–reward expectancies
To get the best from your team, emphasize the anticipated reward value, whether extrinsic or intrinsic. Make sure every individual realizes the link between their performance and the rewards. Even if your organization does not provide performance-based pay, you can bestow other extrinsic rewards, such as allocating more favorable job assignments.

Giving performance feedback
Provide feedback to demonstrate you know what the members of your team are doing and to acknowledge improved performance or a job well done. Especially when individuals are unsure of themselves, you should point out ways in which the person is improving. Praising specific accomplishments will help to bolster that person's self-esteem.

• **Providing salient rewards**
Employees don't all value the same rewards equally, so try to tailor your rewards to get the most out of each individual.

• **Reinforcing the right behavior**
Very often what managers say they want, what they reward, and what they get from their team are somewhat different. If you verbally espouse innovation but reward doing things by the book, you are sending mixed signals and reinforcing the wrong behavior. Think carefully about your rewards and what they mean, and make sure that you reinforce behavior you want to see repeated.

• **Empowering employees to achieve** Empowering the people you are managing, by giving them the authority, information, and tools they need to do their jobs with greater autonomy, can greatly improve their motivation levels.

CHECKLIST MOTIVATING MY TEAM

	YES	NO
• Do I set clear goals and reward success?	☐	☐
• Am I positively reinforcing successful behavior?	☐	☐
• Are the rewards I give salient to each individual I am managing?	☐	☐
• Have I considered linking pay to performance?	☐	☐
• Have I redesigned jobs to help motivate the people doing them?	☐	☐
• Do I make opportunities to learn available to my team?	☐	☐

Appraising performance

As a manager, you must ensure that objectives are met and also that employees learn how to enhance their performance. Providing structured feedback through the formal performance appraisal process can increase productivity and morale and decrease absenteeism and staff turnover.

TIP

KEEP YOUR OPTIONS OPEN

When giving your appraisal, avoid absolutes such as "always" and "never"—if the person you are appraising can introduce one exception to your statement, it can destroy the entire statement's validity and damage your credibility.

Assessing progress

Giving feedback in a formal way in performance appraisal interviews conveys to those you are managing that you care about how they are doing. Appraisals allow you to set goals and monitor achievement, helping to motivate your team to perform to a higher level. They allow you to tell each individual how well they're progressing, which can reinforce good behavior and extinguish dysfunctional behavior. However, the interview itself should be the final step in the performance appraisal process. Appraisal should be a continuous process, starting with the establishment and communication of performance standards. Continually assess how each individual is performing relative to these standards, and use this information to discuss a person's performance with them in the appraisal interview.

? ASK YOURSELF... AM I PREPARED FOR THE APPRAISAL?

- Have I carefully considered the employee's strengths as well as their weaknesses?
- Can I substantiate, with specific examples, all points of praise and criticism?
- Have I thought about any problems that may occur in the appraisal interview?
- Have I considered how I will react to these problems?

Conducting the appraisal interview

Start with the goal of putting the person at ease. Most people don't like to hear their work criticized, so be supportive and understanding and create a helpful and constructive climate. Begin the interview by explaining what will transpire during the appraisal and why. Keep your appraisal goal-oriented, and make sure your feedback is specific. Vague statements provide little useful information. Where you can, get the person's own perceptions of the problems being addressed—there may be contributing factors you are unaware of. Encourage the person to evaluate themselves as much as possible. In a supportive climate, they may acknowledge performance problems independently, thus eliminating your need to raise them. They may also offer viable solutions.

At the end of the interview, ask the recipient to rephrase the content of your appraisal. This will indicate whether or not you have succeeded in communicating your evaluation clearly. Finish by drawing up a future plan of action. Draft a detailed, step-by-step plan for improvement. Include in the plan what needs to be done, by when, and how you will monitor the person's activities.

CONDUCTING APPRAISAL INTERVIEWS

FAST TRACK	**OFF TRACK**
Focusing only on feedback that relates to the person's job	Sharing your feelings about a person's personality
Providing both positive and negative feedback	Focusing your comments only on bad performance
Sharing first-hand observations as evidence	Including rumors and allegations in your appraisal
Being unafraid to criticize the person constructively	Avoiding offending the other person by sugarcoating your criticism

Chapter 4
Leading others

Leadership is the process of providing direction, influencing and energizing others, and obtaining follower commitment to shared organizational goals. Managers need to lead their teams, setting ethical boundaries for them to follow, developing a power base for influencing them to change in positive ways, and helping them improve through coaching and mentoring.

Setting ethical boundaries

Few of us would be likely to steal or cheat, but how principled would you be, or should you be, when faced with routine business situations involving ethical choices? As a leader, you need to have a clear understanding of your ethical principles and set a consistent example for your team.

Understanding ethics

Ethics refer to the rules or principles that define right or wrong conduct. In the workplace, acting ethically is not just an abstraction, it is an everyday occurrence. Consider this dilemma: an employee, after some pressure from you, has found another job. You are relieved because you will not have to fire him; his work has been substandard for some time. But your relief turns to dismay when he asks you for a letter of recommendation. Do you say no and run the risk that he will not leave? Or do you write the letter, knowing that you're influencing someone else to take him on?

Being responsible

Ethics is important for everyone in an organization, particularly because some unethical acts are also illegal. Many organizations want employees to behave ethically because such a reputation is good for business, which in turn can mean larger profits. However, acting ethically is especially crucial for managers. The decisions a manager makes set the standard for those they are managing and help create a tone for the organization. If employees believe all are held to high standards, they are likely to feel better about themselves, their colleagues, and their organization.

Developing ethics

The behavior of managers is under more scrutiny than that of other members of staff, and misdeeds can become quickly and widely known, destroying the reputation of the organization. It is important for managers to develop their own ethical boundaries—lines they and their employees should not cross. To do this, you need to:

Know and understand your organization's policy on ethics.

Anticipate unethical conduct. Be alert to situations that may promote unethical behavior. (Under unusual circumstances, even a normally ethical person may be tempted to act out of character.)

• Consider all consequences. Ask yourself questions such as: "What if my actions were described in detail on a local TV news show, or in the newspaper? What if I get caught doing something unethical? Am I prepared to deal with the consequences?"

• Seek opinions from others. They may have been in a similar situation, or at least can listen and be a sounding board for you.

• Do what you truly believe is right. You have a conscience and are responsible for your behavior. You need to be true to your own internal ethical standards. Ask yourself the simple question: "Can I live with what I have decided to do?"

ASK YOURSELF... IS WHAT I'M ABOUT TO DO ETHICAL?

• Why am I doing what I'm about to do?
• What are my true intentions in taking this action?
• Are there any ulterior motives behind my action, such as proving myself to my peers or superiors?
• Will my actions injure someone, physically or emotionally?
• Would I disclose to my boss or my family what I'm about to do?

Ensuring cultural fit

An organization's culture, or personality, refers to the key characteristics the organization values and which distinguish it from other organizations. Managers need to be aware of organizational culture because they are expected to respond to the dictates of the culture themselves and also to develop an understanding of the culture in those they are managing.

Analyzing organizational culture

The cultural imperatives of an organization are often not written down or even discussed, but all successful managers must learn what to do and what not to do in their organizations. In fact, the better the match between the manager's personal style and the organization's culture, the more successful the manager is likely to be. Founders create culture in three ways. First, they hire and keep employees who think and feel the way they do. Second, founders indoctrinate and socialize these employees to their way of thinking. Third, founders act as role models, and their personality becomes central to the culture of the organization.

Being able to discern an organization's culture is not always a simple task. Many organizations have given little thought to their culture and do not readily display it. To try to find out more about your organization's culture, you might:

Observe the physical surroundings. Look at signs, pictures, styles of dress, length of hair, the degree of openness among offices, and how those offices are furnished and arranged.

Listen to the language. For example, do managers use military terms, such as "take no prisoners," and "divide and conquer"? Or do they speak about "intuition," "care," and "our family of customers"?

Ask different people the same questions and compare their answers. You might ask: how does this company define success? For what are employees most rewarded? Who is on the fast track and what did they do to get there?

Sustaining culture

Managers are responsible for sustaining organizational culture by helping new employees learn and adapt to it. A new worker, for example, must be taught what behaviors are valued and rewarded by the organization, so he or she can learn the "system" and gradually assume those behaviors that are appropriate to their role.

CASE STUDY

Keeping culture consistent

At coffee retailer Starbucks, every employee goes through a set of formal classes during their first few weeks on the job. They are taught the history of the firm, coffee-making techniques, how to explain Starbucks's Italian drink names to baffled customers, and are given coffee-tasting classes. The company's socialization program turns out employees who are well versed in the company's culture and can represent Starbucks's obsession with "elevating the coffee experience" for its customers.

Solving problems

Managerial success depends on making the right decisions at the right times. However, unless you define a problem and identify its root causes, it is impossible to make appropriate decisions about how to solve it. Effective managers know how to gather and evaluate information that clarifies a problem, develop alternatives, and consider the implications of a plan before implementing it.

Identifying problems

A problem exists when a situation is not what is needed or desired. A major responsibility for all managers is to maintain a constant lookout for existing or potential problems, and identify them early before they escalate into serious situations. Managers fulfill this responsibility by keeping channels of communication open, monitoring employees' current performance, and examining deviations from present plans as well as from past experience. Four situations can alert managers to possible problems:

- A deviation from past experience
- A deviation from a set plan
- When other people communicate problems to you
- When competitors start to outperform your team or organization.

The problem-solving process

1 IDENTIFYING
Being conscious of what is going on around you, so you can detect problems early.

2 DEFINING
Making a careful analysis of the problem to be solved, in order to define it as clearly as possible.

Finding solutions

Solving problems involves closing the gap between what is actually taking place and a desired outcome. Once you have identified a problem that needs to be addressed, start by analyzing the problem and defining it as clearly as you can. This is a key step: the definition you generate will have a major impact on all remaining steps in the process. If you get the definition wrong, all remaining steps will be distorted, because you will base them on insufficient or erroneous information. Definition is important even if the solution to the problem appears to be obvious—without a full assessment you may miss an alternative resolution that is more advantageous.

Gather as much information about the situation as you can. Try to understand the goals of all of the parties involved and clarify any aspects of the problem you are unclear about.

Once you are satisfied you have a full understanding of the issues, develop courses of action that could provide a resolution to the problem. There is often more than one way to solve a problem, so it is critical to consider all possible solutions and arrive at several alternatives from which to choose.

Your decision will provide you with an action plan. However, this will be of little value unless it is implemented effectively. Defining how, when, and by whom the action plan is to be implemented and communicating this to those involved is what connects the decision with reality.

Your involvement should not end at implementation, however. Establish criteria for measuring success, then track progress and take corrective actions when necessary. Try to develop and maintain positive attitudes in everyone involved in the implementation process.

4 IMPLEMENTING
Setting your action plan in motion, by creating a schedule and assigning tasks and responsibilities.

MAKING THE DECISION
Evaluating the alternatives and choosing a course of action that will improve the situation in a significant way.

5 FOLLOWING THROUGH
Monitoring progress to ensure the desired outcome is achieved.

Building power

Power is the capacity to influence an individual or group to behave in ways they would not have on their own. Learning how to acquire power and exercise it effectively will help you manage and influence others and develop your managerial career.

Developing power bases

Managerial positions come with the authority to issue directives and allocate rewards and punishments, for example, to assign favorable or unfavorable work assignments, hold performance appraisals, and make salary adjustments. However, you can also build power in other ways:

• Expertise: organizations are often dependent on experts with special skills, such as in technology.
• Charisma: when others admire you and identify with you, you have referent power over them.
• Access to information: possessing information that only you have access to but others need gives you power.
• Association power: having confidantes in powerful positions can increase your power.
• Impression management: shaping the image you project to others in order to influence favorably how others see and evaluate you can give you power. For example, it might be used when lobbying your boss for a pay raise or a promotion.
• Politicking: you don't always win just by being a competent performer. Politicking is taking actions to influence, or attempt to influence, the distribution of advantages and disadvantages within your organization. It involves using strategies to influence decision outcomes in your favor.

REASONING
Use facts and data to make a logical or rational presentation of ideas. This is most effective when others are trustworthy, open, and logical.

HIGHER AUTHORITY
Gain the support of those above you to back your requests. This is effective in bureaucratic organizations where there is great respect for authority.

COALITIONS
Develop support in the organization for what you want to happen. This is most effective where final decisions rely on the quantity, not the quality, of support.

BARGAINING
Exchange benefits or favors to negotiate outcomes acceptable to both parties. This works best when organizational culture promotes give-and-take cooperation.

FRIENDLINESS
Use flattery, create goodwill, act humbly, and be supportive prior to making a request. This works best when you are well liked.

Ways to use managerial power to obtain desired outcomes

SANCTIONS
Use organizationally derived rewards and punishments to obtain desired outcomes. This approach is only for influencing subordinates and may be seen as manipulative.

ASSERTIVENESS
Be direct and forceful when indicating what you want from others. This strategy is most effective when the balance of power is clearly in your favor.

Managing change

Individuals, managers, teams, and organizations that do not adapt to change in timely ways are unlikely to survive in our increasingly turbulent world environment. Managers who anticipate change, learn to adapt to change, and manage change will be the most successful.

Overcoming resistance

Change is the process of moving from a present state to a more desired state in response to internal and external factors. To implement change successfully, you need to possess the skills to convince others of the need for change, identify gaps between the current situation and desired conditions, and create visions for desirable outcomes.

Experienced managers are aware that efforts to change often face resistance. This can be for a variety of reasons, including fear, vested interests, misunderstanding, lack of trust, differing perceptions of a situation, and limited resources. You need to be able to counter this resistance to change through education, participation, and negotiation.

🔍 IN FOCUS... PHASES OF CHANGE

Planned change progresses through three phases:

• **Unfreezing** This involves helping people see a change is needed because the existing situation is undesirable. Existing attitudes and behaviors need to be altered during this phase to reduce resistance, by explaining how the change can help increase productivity, for example. Your goal in this phase is to help the participants see the need for change and to increase their willingness to make the change a success.

• **Changing** This involves making the actual change and requires you to help participants let go of old ways of doing things and develop new ones.

• **Refreezing** The final phase involves reinforcing the changes made so the new ways of behaving become stabilized. If people perceive the change to be working in their favor, positive results will serve as reinforcement, but if not, it may be necessary to use external reinforcements, which can be positive or negative.

Promoting change

Major change does not happen easily. Effective managers are able to establish a sense of urgency that the change is needed. If an organization is obviously facing a threat to its survival, this kind of crisis usually gets people's attention. Dramatically declining profits and stock prices are examples. In other cases, when no current crisis is obvious, but managers have identified potential problems by scanning the external environment, the manager needs to find ways to communicate the information broadly and dramatically to make others aware of the need for change. Managers also have to develop and articulate a compelling vision and strategy people will aspire to, which will guide the change effort. The vision of what it will be like when the change is achieved should illuminate core principles and values that pull followers together. Finally, institutionalizing changes in the organizational culture will refreeze the change. New values and beliefs will become instilled in the culture so employees view the changes as normal and integral to the operations of the organization.

TURN TO THE POSITIVE

Try to use any resistance to your proposed change for your benefit, by making it a stimulus for dialogue and a deeper, more thoughtful analysis of the alternatives.

Helping others improve

Helping employees become more competent is an important part of any manager's job. It contributes to a three-way win for the organization, the manager, and the employees themselves. By helping others resolve personal problems and develop skill competencies—and so help them improve their performance—you will motivate your team to achieve better results for themselves and for the organization.

Diagnosing problems

If you can reduce unsatisfactory performance in the people you are managing, you ultimately make your job easier because you will be increasingly able to delegate responsibilities to them. Unsatisfactory performance often has multiple causes. Some causes are within the control of the person experiencing the difficulties, while others are not.

✓ CHECKLIST **DETERMINING THE CAUSE OF UNSATISFACTORY PERFORMANCE**

	YES	NO
• Is the person unaware their performance is unsatisfactory? If yes, provide feedback.	☐	☐
• Is the person performing poorly because they are not aware of what is expected of them? If yes, provide clear expectations.	☐	☐
• Is performance hampered by obstacles beyond the person's control? If yes, determine how to remove the obstacles.	☐	☐
• Is the person struggling because they don't know how to perform a key task? If yes, provide coaching or training.	☐	☐
• Is good performance followed by negative consequences? If yes, determine how to eliminate the negative consequences.	☐	☐
• Is poor performance being rewarded by positive consequences? If yes, determine how to eliminate the positive reinforcement.	☐	☐

Ways to help others improve

- Ask questions to help discover sources of problems.
- Accept mistakes and use them as learning opportunities.
- Help develop action plans for improvement.
- Seek to educate rather than assist.
- Provide meaningful feedback for learning.
- Encourage continual improvement.
- Demonstrate unconditional positive regard by suspending judgment and evaluation.
- Recognize and reward even small improvements.
- Actively listen to employees and show genuine interest.
- Model the behaviors you desire.

Demonstrating positive regard

The relationship between you and the person you are helping is critical to the success of the coaching, mentoring, or counseling you undertake with them. For a helping relationship to be successful it is important to hold the person being helped in "unconditional positive regard." This means you accept and exhibit warm regard for the individual needing help as a person of unconditional self-worth—a person of value no matter what the conditions, problems, or feelings. If you can communicate positive regard, it provides a climate of warmth and safety because the person feels liked and prized as a person. This is a necessary condition for developing the trust that is crucial in a helping relationship.

Conducting a helping session

Before you speak to someone about how to help them improve their performance, make sure you have acquired all the facts about the situation. Take time to think about what type of help the situation requires and consider how the person might react and how they might feel about what you are going to discuss. During the helping session:

• Start by discussing the purpose of the session.

• Try to make the person feel comfortable and at ease.

• Establish a nondefensive climate, characterized by open communication and trust.

• Before you discuss the problem you have identified, raise and discuss positive aspects of the person's performance.

• Mutually define the problem (performance or attitude).

• Mutually determine the causes. Do not interpret or psychoanalyze behavior; instead, ask questions such as, "What's causing the lack of motivation you describe?"

• Help the other person establish an action plan that includes specific goals and dates.

• Make sure expectations are clearly understood.

• Summarize what has been agreed on.

• Affirm your confidence in the person's ability to make needed changes based on his or her strengths or past history.

After the session, make sure you follow up to see how the person is progressing, and modify the action plan if necessary.

IN FOCUS... FEEDBACK

People need feedback about the consequences of their actions if they are to learn what works and what doesn't and then change their actions to become more effective. Carefully thought-out feedback can increase performance and positive personal development. Applying feedback in the helping process involves:

• Describing observed behaviors and the results and consequences of those behaviors.

• Assessing the impact of the observed behaviors in terms of organizational vision and goals.

• Predicting the personal consequences for the person involved if no changes take place.

• Recommending changes the person could make to improve their behavior.

This sequence of actions applies whether the type of help being given to the person is coaching, mentoring, or counseling.

Counseling others

Counseling is the discussion of emotional problems in order to resolve them or to help the person cope better. Problems that might require counseling include divorce, serious illness, financial problems, interpersonal conflicts, drug and alcohol abuse, and frustration over lack of career progress. Although most managers are not qualified as psychologists, there are several things managers can do in a counseling role before referring someone to a professional therapist.

Confidentiality is of paramount importance when counseling others. To open up and share the reasons for many personal problems, people must feel they can trust you and that there is no threat to their self-esteem or their reputation with others. Emphasize that you will treat in confidence everything the other person says regarding personal matters.

Dealing with personal problems

Getting a person to recognize they have a problem is often the first step in helping them deal with it. You can then follow up by helping them gain insights into their feelings and behaviors, and by exploring the alternatives open to them.

Sometimes people just need a sounding board for releasing tension, which can become a prelude to clarifying the problem, identifying possible solutions, and taking corrective action. Talking things through in a counseling session can help people sort out their feelings into more logical and coherent thoughts.

Above all, be supportive and provide reassurance. People need to know their problems have solutions. If problems are beyond a person's capability to solve, explain how professional treatment can be obtained, through Employee Assistance Programs, for example, or health care plans.

TIP

BE SUPPORTIVE

Reassure those you are counseling that their problems have solutions and that they have the ability to improve their situation.

Coaching and mentoring

Coaching is the process of helping people improve performance. A coach analyzes performance, provides insight on how to improve, and offers the leadership, motivation, and supportive climate to help achieve that improvement. In mentoring relationships, a more experienced person formally pairs up with a less experienced one to help show them "the ropes" and to provide emotional support and encouragement.

HOW TO... COACH A PROCESS

Explain and then demonstrate the process.

Observe the person practicing the process.

Provide immediate, specific feedback.

Express confidence in the person's ability.

Agree on follow-up actions.

Helping others develop

As a coach, a manager's job is to help members of their team develop skills and improve. This involves providing instruction, guidance, advice, and encouragement. Effective coaches first establish a supportive climate that promotes development. It is particularly important you remain nonjudgmental and understanding throughout the process, try to solve problems jointly, and educate those you are coaching about how to solve their own problems in the future. As you learn more about the person you are coaching, try to determine the sources of any problems they are having and provide meaningful feedback.

Mentoring is a broader role. The goal of a mentor is to help a less experienced person achieve his or her career goals. Mentors perform as both coaches and counselors as they guide their less experienced associates toward improved performance. Mentoring can help new organization members gain a better understanding of the organization's goals, culture, and advancement criteria. It can also help them become more politically savvy and avoid potential career traps. As a mentor, try to help others reduce the stress caused by uncertainty about how to do things and deal with challenging assignments. Be a source of comfort when newer, less experienced people just need to let off steam or discuss career dilemmas.

Three key skills for successful coaching

1
FINDING WAYS TO IMPROVE PERFORMANCE

3
CREATING A SUPPORTIVE CLIMATE

Help others improve by observing what they do, asking questions, listening, and crafting unique improvement strategies.

Use active listening, empower others to implement appropriate ideas, and be available for assistance, guidance, and advice.

2
INFLUENCING OTHERS TO CHANGE THEIR BEHAVIOR

Monitor people's progress and development and recognize and reward even small improvements.

Be a role model for the qualities you expect from others, such as openness, commitment, and responsibility.

Involve others in decision-making processes—this helps encourage people to be responsive to change.

Break large, complex projects into series of simpler tasks—this can boost confidence as the simpler tasks are achieved.

Managing careers

In today's rapidly changing business landscape, managers need to manage their careers actively and provide career guidance to those they are managing. To determine where and how you can best contribute, you need to know yourself, continually develop yourself, and be able to ascertain when and how to change the work you do.

Charting your own career path

Self-assessment is an ongoing process in career management. Successful careers develop when people are prepared for opportunities because they know their strengths, their methods of work, and their values. Self-directed career management is a process by which individuals guide, direct, and influence the course of their careers. This requires exploration and awareness of not only yourself, but also your environment. Individuals who are proactive and collect relevant information about personal needs, values, interests, talents, and lifestyle preferences are more likely to be satisfied and productive when searching for job opportunities, to develop successful career plans, and to be productive in their jobs and careers.

🔍 IN FOCUS... CAREER STAGES

Individuals just beginning their careers are usually more concerned with identifying organizations that have the potential to satisfy their career goals and match their values. After settling into a job, focus shifts to achieving initial successes, gaining credibility, learning to get along with their boss, and managing image. Managers in the middle of their careers are more concerned with career reappraisal, overcoming obsolescence brought on by technological advances, and becoming more of a generalist. In the latter stages of their careers, managers focus more on teaching others and leaving a contribution before retirement.

Driving forward

The first step in self-directed career management is planning. Taking your strengths, limitations, and values into account, start searching the environment for matching opportunities. Use the information you gather to establish realistic career goals and then develop a strategy to achieve them. As you progress through your career plan, regularly undertake performance appraisals to make sure you are remaining on track and that your goals haven't changed.

Directing others

The most important thing you can do to contribute to the career development of others is to instill in them the need to take responsibility for managing their own careers. Then you can provide support that will enable those you are managing to add to their skills, abilities, and knowledge in order to maintain their employability within the organization. To help those you are managing develop their careers:

• Keep your team updated about the organization's goals and future strategies so they will know where the organization is headed and be better able to develop a personal career-development plan to share in that future.
• Create growth opportunities for your team, to give them new, interesting, and professionally challenging work experiences.
• Offer financial assistance, such as tuition reimbursement for college courses or skills training.
• Allow paid time off from work for off-the-job training and ensure that those you are managing have reasonable workloads so they are not precluded from having time to develop new skills, abilities, and knowledge.

Index

A

ability 50-1
  measuring 51
  and performance
    188–189
absenteeism 123
abstract reasoning
  51
accountability,
  delegation 186
active listening 40,
  164-5
activities
  business game 55
  case study 55
  chaired discussion
    54
  in-tray exercise 55
  leaderless discussion
    55
  oral presentation 55
  planning 52
  practical task 55
  role play 55
  rules 52
addressing interview
  candidates 26
aggressive behavior
  152
agreements, team
  management 185
Andon system 105

appearance, nonverbal
  communication
  166
applicant tracking
  systems (ATS)
  19
appraisals 192-3
  conducting 98
  elements of 99
aptitude 50-1
  measuring 51
assertiveness 152-3,
  201
assessment centers
  46-7, 63
  history 47
  holding 46–47
  planning 47
association power
  200
assumptions, self-
  awareness 154-5
authority 117, 166-7
  delegation, 186
autonomy, job design
  180-1

B

background screening
  56–57
bargaining
  building power
    201

bargaining cont'd
  tactics 172-3
behavior 96
behavioral spectrum
  63
Belbin, R. Meredith
  91
benchmarking:
  motivating people
    141
Blake-Mouton
  management grid
  97
blame culture 8
body language:
  interviews 52-3
  observing 52–53,
    166–167
  see also nonverbal
    communication
boredom 166
boundaries, ethical
  194–195 brands 18
budget, for interviews
  13, 54
business games 55
bullies 153

C

candidates
  for interview
  preparing for 29
  selecting 24

candidates cont'd
  special needs 27
  tracking 19
career management
  210-11
case studies: interview
  exercises 55
change management
  202-3
  motivation 130-3
  preparation 131
  stages 132, 203
  types 131
change roller coaster
  132-3
charisma 200
checklist
  preparing 12
client relationships 181
closed questions 34,
  35
coaching 107, 128,
  205, 208-9
  skills 129
coalitions: building
  power 201
commitment-based HR
  118
communication 99,
  160-1
  channels 121
  conflicts 174
  and cultural diversity
    177
  developing 120-1
  effective messages
    162-3

communication cont'd
  feedback 170–171
  listening skills
    164–165
  nonverbal cues
    166–167
  positive regard 205
  problem solving 198
  processes 141
  team management
    184
  see also feedback;
    listening skills;
    nonverbal
    communication
competency:
  interviews
    32-3, 44
  measuring 33
competency-based
  questioning 32
confidence 166-7
confidentiality,
  counseling 207
conflict management
  157, 174-5
consulting 124-5
contingency plans:
  interviews 23
cost-to-hire 72
counseling 205,
  207
credentials
  verifying 34
credibility, effective
  messages
    163

crises, managing
  change 203
cultural change 131
cultural concerns
  addressing 37
  corporate dressing
    37
  eating habits 37
  employee
    associations 37
  gestures and eye
    contact 37
  religious facilities
    37
cultural differences:
  interviewing
  people 36-7
cultural diversity
  176–177
cultural fit 196-7
culture
  blame 88
  high performance
    88-9
  positive 88

D

Day One
  planning 75
decision-making
  delegating 187
  interview candidates
    64
  motivating people
    124-5

defensiveness,
nonverbal
communication
167
delegation 155, 186-7
motivating people
126-7
demotivation 122-3
development:
motivating people
107
difficult situations
130-43
discrimination 38-9,
49
dispersed workers
134-5
distributive bargaining
172-3
diversity 176-7
interviewing people
36-7
dress codes 36

E

effective
communication
162-3
electronic
communication
161
emotional intelligence
(EI) 150-1
emotional problems,
counseling 207

empathy 117
empowerment
186
EQ: measuring
emotional
intelligence
150-1
ethics 194-5
ethnic diversity
176-7
exercises
planning 46, 52–55
standardizing 47
structuring 54
expectancy theory
83
expectations 107
experiential learning
168
expertise, building
power 200
extrinsic rewards 190
eye contact 37
active listening
165

F

facial expressions
observing 52–53
feedback 170-1
delegation 187
helping others to
improve 206
interviews 46, 72
job design 180-1

feedback cont'd
motivating people
84, 92, 93, 104,
129
performance
appraisal 192
self-awareness 149
filtering matrix 20,
24
format, interviewing
30–31
at a distance 31
panel 30
team 31
founders,
organizational
culture 196
future
mapping the 75
future team
developing 60

G

gaming 96
gatekeepers 39
gestures 37
globalization, and
diversity 176
goals
aligning 60-1, 85
feedback 170-1
linking 64
mentoring 208
performance
appraisal 192–193

goals cont'd
  personal mission
    statements 24-5
  setting 99, 100,
    114
  stretch 101
  team management
    178-9
Goleman, Daniel
  150
group interview
    activities
  carrying out 52–55
  preparing for 54

H

Herzberg, Frederick
  82, 83
hierarchy of needs
  82, 188-9
high-performance
    culture 88-9
high-performing
    teams 182-5
home workers 134-5
honesty:
  communication
    163
  teaching skills
    169
  team management
    184
hygiene factors 83

I

Iacocca, Lee 182
identity checks 56-7
illegal questions
    38-9
impression
    management 200
in-tray exercises 55
incentives see rewards
individual needs 97
influences 156
information
  as power 200
  background 45
  interviews 27, 44-5
  gathering 44–45
  providing 27
  requesting 68
  sharing 120
informing selectees 66
instrumental values
    157
intangible motivators
    87
integrative bargaining
    172-3
interviewees
  preparing for 29
  selecting 24
  special needs 27
  tracking 19
interviewer
  questioning the 43
interviews
  addressing
    candidates 26

interviews cont'd
  agenda 22
  applicant tracking
    systems (ATS) 19
  assessment centers
    46-7
  body language
    52-3
  budgeting 13
  checklist 12
  concluding 42-3
  contingency
    planning 23
  cultural issues 36-7
  decision-making 64
  discrimination 38-9
  feedback 46
  format 30-1
  group activities
    52-5
  information 27,
    44-5
  inviting candidates
    26-7
  matrix 20-1, 24
  meeting candidates
    29
  nonverbal
    communication
    40-1
  overqualified
    candidates 25
  panel interviews
    30
  performance
    appraisal 192-3
  planning 12-13

interviews cont'd
  preparing to meet
    candidate 29
  questionnaires 26
  questions 32-5,
    38-9, 42
  screening 25, 56-7
  selection 24
  shortlist 24-5
  special needs 27
  timekeeping 22, 34
  venue 28
  video-conferencing
    31
intrinsic rewards 190

J K

job boards 19
job descriptions 14-15
job design 180-1
job offers 66-7
job profile 14–15
job requirements 14
job role 15, 94-5
job rotation 107
job titles 17
journals 149
key performance
    indicators 104

L

labor market:
    diversity
    176

language,
    organizational
    culture 197
lateral thinking 114
leaderless discussion
    exercises 55
leadership skills
    194-211
  building power
    200-1
  career management
    210–211
  coaching and
    mentoring 208-9
  ethics 194-5
  helping others to
    improve 204-7
  managing change
    202-3
  motivating teams
    140
  organizational culture
    196-7
  problem solving
    198–199
learning by
    experience 168
listening skills
    40, 164-5
  interviewing people
    40

M

management styles
    154-5

Maslow, Abraham
    82, 188-9
matrix, creating a
    20–21
  filtering 20, 24
  qualitative 20–21
McGinn, Rich 176
McGregor, Douglas
    84
measurement
  motivation 92-3
  progress 104-5
meeting candidates
    29
mentoring 107, 205,
    208-9
milestones, team
    management 184
mission statements
    158-9
mistakes: learning
    from 114
motivating environment
    80-1
motivation 188-91
  active listening
    165
  cultural diversity
    177
  long-term 96
  management styles
    154-5
  measuring 92-3
  performance
    appraisal 188-9,
    192
  principles 82-3

motivation cont'd
 self-motivation 90,
  112-15
 short-term 96
 teaching skills 169
motivation scorecard
  143
motivators 116-17
 Herzberg's 83
 intangible 87
 tangible 86
mutual trust, team
  management 184
Myers-Briggs Type
  Indicator 48

N

needs
 hierarchy 82, 188-9
 motivating people
  96-7
 true needs 652-3
negotiation 172-3
nervousness, nonverbal
  communication
  166
new recruits 90
 checking credentials
  56
 onboarding 74-5
 screening 25,
  56-7
"noise": in
  communication
  161

nonverbal
 communication
  161, 162, 166-7
 active listening
  165
 cues 166–167
 interviewing people
  40-1

O

objectives
 personal 103
 setting 100-3
 sustainable 103
observation 40–41
offers: job offers
  66-7
onboarding 74-5
online profiles
 exploring 59
open questions
  34, 35
openness
 nonverbal
  communication
  167
 team management
  184
oral communication
  161
oral presentation
 exercises 55
organization
 protecting the
  56–57

organizational culture
  196-7
overqualified
 candidates 25

P

"package"
 building the 66
panel interviews 30
paraphrasing 165
participant–observers,
  team management
  185
passive behavior 152
pay 110-11
performance
 appraisal 192–193
 coaching 208–209
 feedback 170–171,
  191
 helping others to
  improve 204–207
 high-performing
  teams 182–185
 indicators 96,
  104-5
 maximizing 81
 measuring 104-5
 motivation and
  188–189
 paying for 110-11
 recognizing 108-9
 self-esteem and
  133
 supporting 80-1

performance cont'd
targets 169
underperformers
123, 136-7
performance analysis
149
appraisal 192-3
coaching 208-9
feedback 191
helping others to
improve 204-7
high-performing
teams 182-5
motivation 188-9,
192
person specification
16-17
personal goals 103
personal mission
statements 158-9
personal problems
207
personality types 152
physiological needs
189
"Plan B" 23
planning: career
management 211
team management
178–179
politicking 200
politics 121
poor performance
see
underperformers
positive attitude
115

positive regard
205
positive reinforcement
190
posture, nonverbal
communication
166
power building
200-1
practical tasks 55
pre-interview planning
13
problem solving
198-9
motivating people
136-7
professional
assessment 45
professional
qualifications:
acquiring 107
professional skills
50-1
project teams:
motivating
138-9
promotion 119
psychometric tests
criteria 49
understanding 48

Q

qualifications 44,
45, 107
qualitative matrix 20-1

questionnaires:
pre-interview 26
questions
active listening
165
closed 34, 35
competency-based
32-3
hypothetical 35
illegal 38-9
leading 35
open 34, 35
other types 34
personal 38
probing 34, 35
stress 35
teaching skills 169
unusual 34, 35
verification 34, 35

R

recognition 108,
119
recognition systems
108-9
recruitment 90-1
addressing
candidates 26
advertising 73
agenda 22
applicant tracking
systems (ATS) 19
assessment centers
46-7
body language 52-3

recruitment cont'd
  budgeting 13
  checklist 12
  concluding 42-3
  contingency
    planning 23
  cultural diversity
    177
  cultural issues 36-7
  decision-making
    64
  discrimination 38-9
  feedback 46
  format 30-1
  group activities
    52-5
  information 27,
    44-5
  inviting candidates
    26-7
  matrix 20-1, 24
  meeting candidates
    29
  nonverbal
    communication
    40-1
  overqualified
    candidates 25
  panel interviews
    30
  performance
    appraisal 192-3
  planning 12-13
  preparing to meet
    candidate 29
  process 72-3
  questionnaires 26

recruitment cont'd
  questions 32-5,
    38-9, 42
  screening 25, 56-7
  selection 24
  shortlist 24-5
  special needs 27
  timekeeping 22,
    34
  venue 28
  video-conferencing
    31
recruitment process
  reviewing 72
recruitment software
  19
references 68-9
referrals 13
reinforcement, positive
  190
rejection letters
  70-1
relationships
  emotional
    intelligence
    151
  helping others to
    improve 205
  with clients 181
religious facilities
  37
resistance: change
  management
  202
response rate 93
responsibility: career
  management 211

return on investment
  measuring 72
reviews, performance
  183
rewards 190-1
  motivating people
    119
  software 19
role models,
  organizational
  culture 196
role play 55

S
safety needs 189
salary 66, 67,
  83
score sheets 21
screening 25,
  56-7
self-actualization
  189
self-awareness
  148-9
  assertiveness
    152-3
  assumptions
    154-5
  career management
    210
  clarifying your values
    156–157
  emotional
    intelligence
    150-1

self-awareness cont'd
personal mission
statements
158-9
values 156-7
self-esteem 133,
189
self-management
151
self-motivation 90,
112-15
sender credibility
163
setbacks: learning
from 158
shortlists 24-5
skills
job design 180–181
professional 50-1
teaching 168-9
uncovering 44
unexpected 65
SMART goals
159, 179
social awareness
151
social needs 189
social media 18, 58–59
social networking
sites 18, 58-9
software: recruitment
19
spatial reasoning 50,
51
special needs 27
staff absenteeism
123

staff opinion 93
STAR method 32
Starbucks 197
strengths, assessing
62-3
stretch goals 101
Sullivan, John 26
support groups 159
surveys 92-3
sustainable objectives
103

T
targets, performance
169
target-setting 85,
101
tasks: job design
180-1
teaching skills
168-9
team management
178-93
delegation
186-7
developing future
team 60
high-performing
teams 182-5
job design 180-1
motivation 140-1,
188-91
performance
appraisal
192-3

technological aids
using 18–19
telephone calls:
screening
candidates 25
terminal values 157
tests 47, 48-51
theory X management
84
theory Y management
84
time management:
interviewing
people 22
Tom's of Maine
161
training
career management
211
motivating people
106
trust
gaining 117, 142
team management
184

U V
underperformers
123, 136-7
unexpected skills
65
values
clarifying 156-7
conflicts 157
matching 61

alues cont'd
  personal mission
    statements
    158-9
aluing people
  118-19
enues: interviews
  28
erbal techniques see
  communication
etting procedure 57
deo-conferencing
  31
sion, managing
  change 203
sualization:
  assertiveness
    153
room, Victor 83

X Y Z
X-style managers
  154-5
Y-style managers
  154-5
zero-sum conditions
  172

V

ebsite 18, 74
in-win solutions
  172-3
ork hours 66
ork-life balance
  115
ork needs 97
orking conditions
  83
orking hours 66
ritten communication
  161
rong moves
  avoiding 39

Author Biographies

MANAGING PEOPLE

Johanna S. Hunsaker is Professor of Management and Organizational Behavior, and Team Leader of the Management, Leadership, and Ethics Group in the School of Business Administration at the University of San Diego. She has been on the faculty at San Diego State University, the University of Wisconsin–Milwaukee, and has taught in France, Germany, Spain, Hong Kong, and Saipan. Dr. Hunsaker has published more than 50 articles on management and organization topics, and a book on gender issues in the workplace, *Strategies and Skills for Managerial Women*. Her consultancy work focuses on gender-related issues in the workforce, especially with reference to sexual harassment and gender discrimination. Her clients include Security Pacific Finance Corporation, San Diego Community College District, the United States Border Patrol, the Australian and New Zealand Institutes of Management, Episcopal Community Services, the San Diego Zoological Society, Naval Personnel Command, the Brooktree Corporation, several law firms, and General Dynamics.

Phillip L. Hunsaker is Professor of Management in the School of Business Administration at the University of San Diego. He has been a faculty member at Bond University, University of Wisconsin–Milwaukee, California State University Northridge, University of Southern California, University of California San Diego, and Ahlers Center for International Business in Paris, Rome, Munich, Barcelona, and Prague. He consults for many international organizations including Coca-Cola, Qualcomm, Atlantic Richfield, General Dynamics, J.I. Case Co, Mead-Johnson, Boston Scientific, and American Honda. Dr. Hunsaker has authored more than 100 articles on management and organization behavior. He has so far written 14 books including *The New Art of Managing People*; *Management: A Skills Approach*; *Training in Interpersonal Skills*; *Communication at Work*; *Training in Management Skills*; *The Dynamic Decision Maker*; *Management and Organizational Behavior* (European edition); *You Can Make It Happen: A Guide to Personal and Organizational Change*; and *Strategies and Skills for Managerial Women*.

MOTIVATING PEOPLE

Mike Bourne is Professor of Business Performance and Director of the Centre for Business Performance at Cranfield School of Management in the UK. After spending 15 years in industry, Mike gained his Ph.D. at Cambridge University and has spent the last 15 years helping companies design, develop, and use balanced scorecards and performance-management systems. He has worked with and consulted for companies including Accenture, Amadeus, BAe Systems, European Central Bank, Lloyds TSB, McCormick Europe, NHBC, Oki Europe, PWC, Schering, Thales, Tube Lines, Unilever, and Wolseley. He has authored more than 100 publications and is a regular conference presenter and workshop leader. Mike is also a Chartered Management Accountant and a Chartered Engineer.

Pippa Bourne is Regional Director, East England, for the Institute of Chartered Accountants in England and Wales. She gained her MBA from Aston Business School and her early career was in marketing. She then moved into management development, running profit-making training businesses over many years at the Chartered Institute of Management Accountants, City University Business School, and the Chartered Institute of Management. Her recent interest has been in developing strategic processes for measuring and managing business sustainability. She has authored five books and coedited the journal *Measuring Business Excellence.* Pippa is a Chartered Marketer.

INTERVIEWING PEOPLE
DeeDee Doke is the editor of the semimonthly business-to-business magazine and leading UK recruitment industry title *Recruiter*, and its online sister *recruiter.co.uk*. She launched the related title *Resourcing* and has written on human resources and recruitment issues for numerous magazines and daily newspapers.

Acknowledgments

Original editions produced for DK by

cobaltid
www.cobaltid.co.uk
Editors: Louise Abbott, Kati Dye,
Maddy King, Sarah Tomley, Marek Walisiewicz
Designers: Darren Bland, Claire Dale,
Paul Reid, Annika Skoog, Lloyd Tilbury,
Shane Whiting

DK India
Editors: Ankush Saikia, Saloni Talwar
Designers: Ivy Roy
Design Manager: Arunesh Talapatra

DK UK
Peter Jones (Senior Editor), Daniel Mills
(Project Editor), Helen Spencer (Senior Art
Editor), Adèle Hayward (Executive Managing
Editor), Kat Mead (Managing Art Editor), Ben
Marcus (Production Editor), Sonia Charbonnier
(Creative Technical Support), Stephanie
Jackson (Publisher), Peter Luff (Art Director).

The publisher would like to thank Yvonne
Dixon for indexing, Constance Novis for
Americanization, and Margaret Parrish
for proofreading.

Picture credits
The publisher would like to thank the
following for their kind permission to
reproduce their photographs:

(Key: a—above, b—below, c—center, l—left,
r—right, t—top.)

8 Constantine Chagin; 10 IMAGEMORE Co.,
Ltd.; 15 Ravi Tahilramani; 17 Getty Images:
George Diebold; 23 cb Zac Macaulay; 23
bc Corbis: Randy Faris; 24 iStockphoto.
com; 30 Image Source; 32 Marc Dietrichc;
36 Ted Horowitz; 41 George Cairns; 48 Mads
Abildgaard; 49 Vasiliy Yakobchuk; 53 bl, br, tl
Yunus Arakon; 53 cl, cr, tr Sergejs Cunkevics;
57 Paul Taylor; 62 Thom Lang; 66 Coneyl Jay;
70 Darren Robb; 72 Luis Pedrosa; 76 Corbis:
James W. Porter; 78 Getty Images: Zia Soleil;
81 iStockphoto.com: Ethan Myerson; 84 Corbis:
Frédérik Astier; 86 Getty Images: Werner
Dieterich; 88 Getty Images: Digital Vision; 90
Corbis: Cultura/Corbis (cl), Getty Images: Susan
Vogel (fbl), Brad Wilson (clb); 91 Corbis: Cultura
Limited (c), Harry Vorsteher (ca), Getty Images:
Rainer Elstermann (cra), Frank van Groen (crb),
Jed Share/Kaoru Share (tr), Anthony Strack (tc),
Chev Wilkinson (cr), Hideki Yoshihara (cb); 92
iStockphoto.com: Kanstantsin Shcharbinski;
98 Getty Images: Scott Kleinman; 99 Corbis:
William Whitehurst (ftr); 102 Corbis: Steve Allen;
107 Getty Images: David Sacks; 109 Corbis:
Solus-Veer; 113 iStockphoto.com: Sebastiaan
de Stigter; 115 Getty Images: Medioimages/
Photodisc; 118 Getty Images: Tanya Zouev;
122 Getty Images: Kevin Summers; 126 Getty
Images: Hans Neleman; 132 Corbis: So Hing-
Keung; 138 Corbis: Bruce Benedict; 140 Corbis:
Tony Kurdzuk/Star Ledger; 144 Getty Images:
Stephen Swintek; 146 Getty Images: Mike
Powell; 153 Alamy Images: Jose Luis Stephens;
159 Alamy Images: artpartner-images.com; 167
Alamy Images: Horizon International Images
Limited; 170 Getty Images: Jetta Productions;
176 iStockphoto.com: Stefanie Timmermann;
181 iStockphoto.com: Todd Harrison; 182 Alamy
Images: Sarah Weston; 186 iStockphoto.com:
Jasmin Awad; 196 Getty Images: Chad Baker;
200 Alamy Images: David Wall; 202 Alamy
Images: Steve Bloom Images; 204 iStockphoto.
com: imagedepotpro; 209 iStockphoto.com:
Jamie Otterstetter; 210 iStockphoto.com:
Evgeny Kuklev.